How to Pray Heaven on Earth

Judith Butler

New Wine Press

New Wine Press
PO Box 17
Chichester
England PO20 6YB

All Scripture quotations are taken from the New King James Version of the Bible, copyright © 1983 by Thomas Nelson, Inc., Nashville, USA.

ISBN: 1 903725 04 6

Typeset by CRB Associates, Reepham, Norfolk.
Printed in England by Clays Ltd, St Ives plc.

Contents

Acknowledgements

This is a great opportunity to show my gratitude to those who have made this book possible. Firstly, I want to thank the leadership of Kingdom Faith for their input into my life over the last ten years. This is part of the fruit! Then there is an 'army' of people who have prayed and supported me in the work. I am so grateful for you all. Specifically, thanks to Joan Brooke for faithfully praying, Jeremy and Jane Butler and Romolo and Myriam Giovanardi for their faithful support. Finally, I am indebted to Andrea Browne, my friend and ministry partner these last six years. Thanks for everything, especially the wisdom and encouragement. You never let me give up and have given me such joy as we have shared in the work of the Kingdom.

About the Author

Judith Butler is presently pastoring a church in the South West of England. Her dynamic ministry of preaching and teaching the Word has taken her to parts of Africa, America and more extensively Europe, where she has seen God's power save and transform many lives. Judith is a pastor at Kingdom Faith Ministries and has led the prayer school there for the last seven years where Pastor Colin Urquhart is director. She preaches the Word with authority and revelation and her greatest passion is to see every believer empowered and motivated to pray and 'go into all the world'. She brings God's message in a way that encourages faith and vision to see the Lord do great things in this generation.

Foreword

What is the point of praying unless you get results? Judith Butler has a very powerful ministry of teaching and leading others in prayer. She has been gifted by God with the ability to motivate others to become praying people, showing them that prayer should be both exciting and rewarding.

This is much more than a book on prayer. With great clarity you will be led step by step into a place of greater faith in God, enabling you to enter into a real and living relationship with Him. You need to know the One to Whom you pray.

Judith Butler covers an amazing amount of ground, giving you the essence of the truth that you need to know, but without wearying you with unnecessary detail! Having laid this good foundation of faith and relationship, she shows you how to approach God so that your prayer life will be both fulfilling and effective. This short book gives clear teaching on how to depend on God's Holy Spirit in prayer, and how to exercise authority over the adverse, negative tactics of the enemy.

How to Pray Heaven on Earth is a book by someone with a proven international ministry that will help any who want to pray more effectively. If you are one of those people who feels a failure at prayer, this is the ideal book for you. It will show you how, by applying simple principles, you can have an effective relationship with God in prayer.

Even if you have been a Christian for many years, there is plenty here that will enrich your prayer life, taking you to a place of greater faith in which you expect God to hear and answer you!

Knowing Judith Butler over many years, and having witnessed the fruit of her ministry, I believe *How to Pray Heaven on Earth* will be an important book to which you will want to refer again and again.

Colin Urquhart
Kingdom Faith
April 2001

Introduction

God is changing the shape of this world through the prayers of His people. He is moving and working through Christians who are praying His will and Kingdom into every situation and circumstance.

However, many Christians today face considerable discouragement and even apathy in prayer. They struggle to succeed and enjoy this vital part of their life with God and are weak because of it.

This book will encourage and stimulate every believer to see and access the wonderful resources made available to us in Christ. It is practical by nature and full of teaching with revelation that will bring you understanding on how to pray effectively. Each chapter has a section which can be used either for personal or group application.

God wants us to have answers to our prayers! I believe that as you read these pages, the Holy Spirit will revive your vision and faith for a joyful and fruitful prayer life. It is my prayer that the Lord be glorified through your prayers, and as a result, demonstrate who He is to the world.

Chapter 1

Connecting with God

What is prayer?

I want to begin this book by defining and laying some foundations on the subject of prayer. I hope that you will catch how simple, and yet how profound, prayer is. For a Christian, prayer is to be as natural as breathing and just as vital for life!

Prayer is communication between man and God

God created man to have fellowship or share life with Him and gave every individual ever born an inherent desire to know Him. Discovering what we are created for and why is the path to fulfilment and joy in our lives. Communication with God brings us into our destiny. Through prayer we get to know God and begin to understand why we were created.

A few years ago, a powerful film was made about the life of a Scottish athlete called Eric Liddell. He was a Christian and one of the greatest runners of his time. When he ran, he knew that he was fulfilling part of his destiny – he'd been designed and created for that purpose. I remember during the film that he spoke about the joy he experienced whilst running. He said he would reach a certain point in a race when he would run solely for the glory of God. Each one of us has a special, God-given purpose and destiny and the way we discover it is through knowing God and His will for our lives! This comes from being in relationship with Him and the joy of knowing God and living for His pleasure awaits every one of us.

God enjoys our company!

The Bible shows us an amazing and life-changing truth. It is God's desire and intention to communicate with man! All through the ages God has been calling man to Himself, so strong is His love for us. He actually wants to communicate with us and enjoy our company. This relationship is based on His unfailing and perfect love for us. We can now enter into the most exciting, fulfilling relationship of our lives.

Our relationship with God is only possible because He initiated it! We love Him because He first loved us (1 John 4:19).

Knowing God through His Word

God's Word shows us His character and will. We must be careful not to make God in our own image, based on our experiences in life or man's opinion. Prayer is to be based on revelation of the character and will of God through His Word.

Have you noticed that our impressions of God can be shaped or influenced by our experiences in life? I know that when I first became a Christian, it was difficult for me to accept that it is God's will to heal the sick. My experience did not match up with God's Word and so I based my opinion on what I had seen. I remember having rather heated discussions with other Christians about this subject. They believed in God's will to heal and trusted His Word. I wanted proof! I have since changed my opinion (thank God) and have chosen to believe God's Word and not my experiences.

Prayer is strong and effective when we pray based on the revelation of God's Word.

Receiving from God

Most of us also know that by asking in prayer we can receive God's help and provision. Children have such a lot to teach us about prayer and relationship with God. When they ask for a drink they expect to receive it! And if they don't get it the first time they ask, then they will continue asking until they do. I remember taking my five-year-old niece on a three-hour car journey. Within five minutes of leaving the house, she was asking for a drink of water. Incredible, as she had only just had a drink a moment before. For the sake of my own sanity I had to stop the car and provide for her request, otherwise I would be hearing nothing else for the entire journey!

Jesus told us to ask, seek and knock until we receive what we ask. This is something we adults need to practise a little more in our prayers – pray until we get it! Of course, the effectiveness of our prayer is based on knowing what God is willing to give. He will not give what is against His will. However, Scripture shows us that God desires to give good things to us. He loves us more than earthly parents love their children, and is willing to provide for our every need. We are created to know God's power working in our lives way beyond any natural power. When we need help, we can call on Him and He answers us with supernatural power. He cares for us and shows His love, answering our prayers!

So, to begin to understand what prayer is we can say – **prayer is life with God** – knowing Him and His provision in our lives and on the earth. This joy of discovering friendship with God and power through prayer will take commitment both in time and lifestyle for any believer, but the rewards are endless. God has called us to Himself in Christ to know Him and to receive from Him all He longs to give.

Why does God require us to pray?

Have you ever wondered why God waits for us to ask Him for things He has already decided to give? When Jesus was teaching His disciples about prayer, He said that God already knows what we need before we ask.

> ' . . . *for your Father knows the things you have need of before you ask Him.'* (Matthew 6:8)

It is comforting to know that our needs never take God by surprise! He knows everything about us down to the finest detail. Recently I asked the Lord to provide for a weekend away somewhere. Due to a busy ministry schedule, I hadn't been able to have a break for a while. It was such a wonderful surprise when a friend called me and said that she had two tickets spare to go to Paris for the weekend. I really never expected such a great answer to this prayer. We need to always keep in mind that He is interested and cares about every part of our lives.

So, if God knows what we need, why doesn't the provision just fall into our laps? Surely, the One who loves us so much should automatically provide for us? And yet He says that we must **ask**, so that we can receive!

Well, one of the reasons we need to ask is that He wants us to involve Him in every aspect of life. It's relationship that He desires. If we didn't go to Him with our requests, we would soon become self-dependent and not develop or grow to depend on Him.

But, there is another reason. We need to go back to the beginning and see God's plan for Adam to understand from Scripture why God requires us to pray. Here we see a key that will help us to understand God's intention to work **with** and **through** us to oversee His creation here on earth. Let these truths impact your heart and mind as you read.

God's original plan

> *'For by Him all things were created that are in heaven and that are on the earth, visible and invisible, whether thrones or dominions or principalities or powers. All things were created through Him and for Him.'*   (Colossians 1:16)

We know from Scripture that God existed before anything was made and that He is the only Creator. Genesis 1:31 tells us that everything He made in the heavens and earth was very **good**. He didn't create bad or sub-standard things. This truth is so important for us to grasp and receive deep into our hearts. The devil lies to man about the intention of God to do good to mankind and to give good things.

God's will for the earth and for man was and is good. We

are to **know** and be fully persuaded that God wants to bless us and do us good.

However, we see much evidence in the world around us that God's will and desire to bless man is not yet fully demonstrated here on earth as it is in heaven. Heaven is a place that is free from sin, sickness and any negative or evil power. It is full of the goodness of God. **Heaven is God's standard and will for the earth**. Yet we can see the evidence of other powers and influences that are at work here on earth. God's will is not yet fully established. We are frequently being made aware of the pain and suffering, injustice and sin throughout the world.

Why? And where does it all come from? Well, Scripture is clear that this is the consequence of man's sin (the fall) and the work of the devil.

Mankind to rule the earth

> *'Then God said, let us make man in our image, according to our likeness, let them have dominion over the fish of the sea, over the birds of the air, and over all the earth and over every creeping thing that creeps on the earth.'* (Genesis 1:26)

After God had made everything He **gave** authority to Adam, the first man ever created. God decided to delegate the responsibility of managing the earth to mankind. Psalm 8:6 tells us that he was made ruler over the works of God's hands. Adam was to have dominion on earth in a way that would bless and nurture God's good creation. He was to keep God's order on earth by overseeing His work.

Authority lost

Even though man originally had the right and authority to rule the earth, Satan tempted Adam and Eve to sin. Once sin entered the human race man lost this God-given right to rule, giving Satan certain rights and power on earth. The entrance of sin gave the devil the opportunity he wanted – to rob, kill and destroy the good that God had made (John 10:10).

Due to man's sin, the devil has gained certain powers in this world, although let's keep in mind that his power is very limited in comparison to the power of God. 2 Corinthians 4:4 tells us that Satan is called *'the god of this age'* and Jesus referred to him as *'the ruler of this world'* (John 12:31).

We know that God is Supreme ruler over all, including the devil. But we also see that God has chosen man to bring His dominion on earth. The revelation every believer needs to be clear about is that God has not changed His original plan to rule the earth through man!

Authority restored – in Christ

God sent His Son Jesus to destroy the works of the devil and to redeem man through His blood sacrifice on the Cross. Man was given authority to rule the earth again, but this time in the Name and power of Jesus and not in his own strength or power. This authority in Christ is greater than the authority Adam was given.

> *'For if by the one man's offence death reigned through the one, much more those who receive abundance of grace and the gift of righteousness will reign in life through the One, Jesus Christ.'*   (Romans 5:17)

Every person who receives Jesus as Lord has been made righteous before God and is given authority over all the power of the enemy. Now we who belong to Him stand in His authority and are called to represent Jesus and bring His rule here on this earth.

> *'Behold, I give you the authority to trample on serpents and scorpions, and over all the power of the enemy, and nothing shall by any means hurt you.'*   (Luke 10:19)

A believer has power to reign **now** in this life through Jesus – in His power and authority. God has chosen to bring His will to the earth through the prayers and authority of His people.

Jesus rules through our prayers

The Kingdom of God comes to the earth as we agree with God's will and ask for it to be done. Prayer really is the greatest power there is on this earth simply because it releases the power of God. God desires to bless and fill the earth with His presence and power, we believe and agree in prayer and He does it. The amazing thing is that He has chosen to execute His will with and through us, not independently from us!

I know this is a well-used example, but it does describe the results of our prayers in a way we can grasp easily. My garden will become overgrown and messy if I don't manage it properly. If I want flowers in it then I will have to plant them. If I want the lawn to look good then I have to cut the grass. If the weeds are left to grow with the other plants, there will be competition for the soil and my flowers will become weak! I might dream about having a beautiful garden, but unless I take action, it will never happen.

If we desire the Kingdom of God to come into our world, we need to co-operate with God and ask for His will to be done. Through prayer we can 'plant' the right things into the earth. If the enemy is ruining our lives and the lives of other people then we have authority to evict him.

God wants us to pray so that He can rule the earth through us and bring His riches and blessing into a world that is desperate to receive from Him.

Note:
The Bible is very clear that we don't wrestle against flesh and blood but against Satan and his kingdom (Ephesians 6:12). We are to rule over the works of the devil and apply our authority through faith in God's Word and prayer. This will advance the Kingdom of God and defeat all the powers of darkness.

Here is one example of bringing the reign of God on earth: A few years ago a friend and I were talking one night to a girl about Jesus. It was getting late and my friend decided to go upstairs to bed. I continued to talk about Jesus and the girl began to describe a vision that God was giving her. She saw a pair of scales with one side weighed down by darkness and the other by light. She knew that her life was in the balance and knew that it was her decision that would determine the way the scales would fall. She was seeing into the spirit realm where there was a battle going on for her soul.

Upstairs my friend wasn't sleeping but on her knees praying. She was operating in the unseen realm and commanding the enemy to loose his hold over this girl's life. As my friend prayed for her salvation, the girl began to respond to Jesus. She gave her life to Christ that night and came out of the kingdom of darkness and into the Kingdom of Light. We had both brought the rule of God to the earth through our words and prayers.

Please understand that we cannot override a person's will through prayer. God has given every person free will to choose life or death. However, we have power to stop the enemy from influencing people's lives and can release God's power. Then people are free to see Jesus and make their own decision to follow Him.

Our battle is not against people but against satanic powers that want to keep people in bondage and darkness. Declaring victory and using our authority in this particular situation over the enemy ultimately brought about the reign of Jesus in this girl's life.

Reigning in life

At times, circumstances and people may be used by the enemy to work against us. Here, we really must be careful not to take offence, but walk in forgiveness and perceive that it is the enemy operating through people. Jesus tells us in His Word to bless our enemies and pray for those who persecute us. In these situations, we are to take authority and rule over these evil powers working through people. Ruling in the Name of Jesus, representing His will and character, we enforce the victory of the Cross over every power of darkness. People and circumstances will change as we begin to exercise our authority over the power of the enemy.

I remember once being with a person who unexpectedly began to get very angry with me. There really was no natural reason for this. The situation began to get quite dangerous and violent. Very quietly, almost under my breath I said, 'In Jesus' Name I bind every spirit of violence and anger.' The person immediately became quiet and began to apologise, saying that they didn't know what had happened! I knew that the reign of God had come.

The Bible tells us that the Kingdom of God is righteousness, peace and joy in the Holy Spirit (Romans 14:17). So, we can say that if God's Kingdom is asked for, these wonderful attributes will be present.

Jesus taught us to pray:

> *'Thy kingdom come, thy will be done on earth, as it is in heaven.'* (Luke 11:2)

Scripture also tells us that God has made us all kings in Christ (Revelation 1:6). A king is someone who rules for God, bringing His righteousness, peace and joy into the earth! We have authority to bring God's rule and Kingdom through our prayers and to evict the enemy by using our authority. Just as Adam had the task of managing the earth for God, so now every believer is to rule on earth in Jesus' Name. This means that we bring the life and victory of Jesus through our lives and into every situation we face. God waits for us to **ask** and **act** in accordance with His will so that His dominion and rule comes to earth through us.

Christians don't rule by their own will but by God's revealed will. God wills something – we agree and ask for it – He does it! Yes, He has power to do everything without us, but the amazing thing is that He has chosen to do it with and through us.

The Lord wants His people to rule the earth in His Name, representing His character, will and authority. He waits for us to ask before He acts on earth. Of course, He will only respond when we ask according to His will. The truth is, if we don't ask, we don't get and the world will not receive the blessing and life God wants to give.

We are like an army, having authority over the powers of darkness, (not over people) implementing and enforcing the will of God through our prayers and through the declaration of His Word. In His Name we evict the powers of darkness and bring in the rule of the Kingdom of God.

Wherever God's people understand this and act on it, the kingdom of darkness is overcome by the Kingdom of Light and there is a very real victory brought to the earth through the prayers and actions of the saints.

Your prayers count!

Many believers are waiting for God to do something and have the ungodly attitude – 'que sera sera – whatever will be will be'. This is not the will of God. We are called to be active and not passive, to ask in faith and receive whatever we ask in agreement with His will.

Everything has already been done for us on the Cross. Our work is to believe, ask and receive! If we see unrighteousness and injustice in our nation, we are not to ignore it, complain or feel helpless. In every situation, including the most difficult ones, Jesus is the answer and we have power to bring in His rule and Kingdom. We are made **kings** and are to behave as such, serving the **King of kings**, bringing change to our nations. We must agree with God's will, not the circumstances, trends or worldly powers, and thereby be the agents of change that God has designed us to be.

Releasing the greatest power there is

We have influence and favour with the Supreme Power of earth and heaven. Many things are happening in our nation that are not the will of God, and we are called by God to bring His Kingdom into every area of society. Prayer will change governments and laws. Prayer will decrease violence in our cities, bringing peace and prosperity, salvation and restoration.

A friend of mine was prayer-walking the streets where he lives. (This means simply to pray as you walk, believing that you are claiming the territory for God – see Joshua 1:3.) Unknown to him, he was being watched over a period of months by a Muslim man. One day this man stopped him to ask what he was doing. My friend explained that he was a Christian and was praying for the people who lived in the area. The man commented that he and his friends had noticed that there was less violence and far more peace in the streets since he had begun to prayer walk.

It's so exciting to be living in these days. I recently watched a documentary showing how God's power is moving in certain cities in the world. Christians have begun to believe God and pray in faith for their communities. Radical changes are taking place with thousands being saved. The reports from the police are amazing. Crime has decreased so much in some places they have closed the prisons. In one city, a drug cartel with a multi-million dollar turnover has broken up and the ringleaders arrested. The number of murders in the city has dropped significantly, with many people coming to Christ and added to the church. In some places up to 80% of the town are saved.

Nothing will be impossible as we pray, believing that great things will happen.

Understand that Satan is only too willing to rule if we let him. One of his most powerful weapons is complacency. We must rise up in Jesus' Name and refuse to accept the devil's influence.

Believe that Jesus has given you the Holy Spirit – the **ruling** Spirit – to evict the work of the devil. Jesus won the war. He has triumphed over the enemy and we are **enforcing His victory**, bringing it into our lives, families and nations! Nothing will be impossible for those who believe. The more we believe and pray, the more the Kingdom of God will advance and the more glory Jesus receives!

Jesus will rule the earth through our lives and prayers. We are in an important position of authority in Christ and must use this position to manage the earth for Him.

Application

1. Thank God for the relationship you have with Him through the sacrifice of Jesus on the Cross. You have been made one with Him and are called to know Him.

2. Thank Him for the ways He has already heard and answered your prayers. Remember the miracles He has done for you with thanksgiving.

3. Believe that He wants to rule the earth through you. Meditate on Psalm 8:6 and Genesis 1:26 – asking God for faith and revelation of His will.

4. Ask Him to show you how to bring His Kingdom into your life, family, workplace and nation. In what way or area is Satan attempting to kill, steal or destroy the good you know God wants to give? Identify this and then pray specifically into those areas.

5. See with the eyes of faith the rule of the Kingdom of God in every area – **as it is in heaven** (righteousness, peace and joy in the Holy Spirit).

Chapter 2

Solid Foundations for Prayer

To have an effective prayer life we need to understand the importance of the work of the Cross. If we pray knowing where we stand with God we will begin from a firm foundation and build on truth.

A wise builder will make sure his foundations are firm and secure so that everything else that is added to that building will have the support and strength to stand. Likewise, we enter into the benefits of God's Kingdom when we build our prayer lives on the firm foundation of truth. Prayers based on anything other than God's Word will not produce the results that we need or that God wants to give. Knowing our position in relation to the enemy will also enable us to overcome his accusations and lies.

This chapter will bring fresh revelation of the work of the Cross and show how we can apply these transforming truths as we pray.

The power of the blood of Jesus

The blood of Jesus carries amazing power for everyday life and enables us to live in victory. Applying faith in the blood will transform your prayers and give you confidence and boldness before God.

> 'Jesus answered and said to them, "This is the Work of God, that you believe in Him whom He sent."'   (John 6:29)

The Lord is always working faith into our hearts so that we believe in all that He has done. Faith is His way for us and this scripture shows us clearly that it is our job to believe. What a challenge for us all! Believe in Jesus and all He accomplished on the Cross and this will bring God's will here on earth. Prayers of faith based on the finished work of the Cross will be prayers that are answered.

Your acceptance is based on His performance

God's acceptance of us is not based on our own performance or ability to live a good life, neither is it based on our character and works. Our standing before God is solely and entirely based on Jesus' work on the Cross for us. This brings absolute freedom into our lives when we believe in the perfect performance of the Son of God and **not** our own.

> *'I am the way, the truth, and the life. No one comes to the Father except through Me.'*   (John 14:6)

The only way to God is through Jesus, His Son. He poured out His blood on the Cross for our sins and the sins of the whole world. Sin entered the human race through Adam, and man was no longer able to fellowship with God, whose nature is holy. Man died spiritually through sin and was destined for eternal separation from God.

Jesus came to the earth and was the perfect, sinless sacrifice required by God to pay for our sins. The gift of **life**, eternal life, is now given to all who believe in Jesus and confess Him as Lord. We are reconciled by Jesus to the Father and adopted as His children.

> *'But as many as received Him, to them He gave the right to become children of God, to those who believe in His Name: who were born not of blood, nor of human flesh, nor of the will of man, but of God.'*   (John 1:12–13)

His blood makes us holy

God's qualification of acceptance is holiness. Not one of us has lived a holy life and without Jesus we have no power to change. However, the good news is Jesus shed His blood on our behalf to make us holy. This is the message of mercy and grace, the work of God and not man!

> *'But this Man* [Jesus]*, after He had offered one sacrifice for sins forever, sat down at the right hand of God ... For by one offering He has perfected forever those who are being sanctified.'* (Hebrews 10:12 & 14)

Because of the sin-state of mankind we could not simply be modified or slightly altered. We had to be made completely new through the sacrifice of the Son of God. This is the only way we can come before God, as new creatures in Christ Jesus.

> *'Therefore, if anyone is in Christ, he is a new creation; old things have passed away; behold, all things have become new.'* (2 Corinthians 5:17)

> *'I have been crucified with Christ; it is no longer I who live, but Christ lives in me; and the life which I now live in the flesh I live by faith in the Son of God, who loved me and gave Himself for me.'* (Galatians 2:20)

We now live by faith in Jesus and His finished work on the Cross. Our sin nature – the old person – has been crucified with Christ. We are now new creatures and made new by Him. We are not **trying** to be someone new – we are. We don't **try** to be made holy by our efforts or works, we **are** made holy by His blood.

> *' ... just as He chose us in Him before the foundation of the world, that we should be holy and without blame before Him in love ... '* (Ephesians 1:4)

Prayer, worship and intimacy with God would not be possible without the shed blood of Jesus and our faith in His work on the Cross. Jesus has made the way for us to come before Him and has clothed us in His righteousness. We are made holy to enjoy fellowship with our Holy God.

'For He made Him who knew no sin to be sin for us, that we might become the righteousness of God in Him.'

(2 Corinthians 5:21)

Faith makes all the difference

Many Christians find themselves unable to approach God with confidence because they think that they are unworthy and unwanted in God's presence. An older lady once approached me during a meeting to ask me a few questions about prayer. She said, 'Judith, you seem to have this prayer thing working for you. I don't have the confidence or ability to pray like you do, I feel so inadequate. When I pray I feel like God isn't there and my prayers seem to bounce off the ceiling and come back to me. I never feel accepted and am so aware of my failures as I pray. I know that I should pray but it really isn't a time I enjoy. What can you do to help me?'

This dear lady had gone through years of her Christian life and not had revelation about the power of the blood of Jesus. The only way I could help her was to tell her about the work of Jesus, and show her that her job was to believe that He had accepted her, cleansed her with His blood and promised to be with her always.

Never are we to base our relationship with God on our feelings as they can vary from one minute to the next. Our prayers may seem to hit the ceiling, but the truth is that God is listening and hearing all the faith-filled prayers of His children. It really does help if we ignore our feelings and thank God that He **is** there as promised and that He **has** made us worthy in His sight.

Only faith in the blood of Jesus makes us worthy. For us to enjoy being with God we must know that we are welcome and not condemned by God. He doesn't constantly remind us of our sins and failures, but reminds us of His mercy and forgiveness. God wipes out our sin – it's the devil that reminds us of our failures.

Early on in my Christian life I did not believe that I was made holy and would try to please God by what I did. Not surprisingly, this resulted in striving and feelings of failure. Then I had this life-changing revelation – Jesus did it all for me so that I can rest in His work. Peace and joy filled my heart! Instead of looking away from Him, feeling guilty and unworthy, I knew I was cleansed and clothed in His right-eousness. He has removed the shame of my sin and I could enjoy His love and acceptance. This changed the way I saw myself and had a positive effect on all my relationships. I became secure in His love, confident that He actually enjoyed me being there with Him.

Faith says, 'God has done it' and accepts like a child.

Daily cleansing from sin

Of course we daily need His mercy and forgiveness. Scripture tells us that His mercies are new **every** morning. We aim to please Him with our lives, but if we fail we only need to ask Him to forgive our sin and He removes it.

> *'If we confess our sins, He is faithful and just to forgive us our sins and to cleanse us from all unrighteousness.'*
>
> (1 John 1:9)

Confessing every known sin and turning away from it brings a believer back into right relationship with God.

Application

1. Believe that Jesus is the only way to the Father. Confess Him as your Lord.

2. Believe that you are born of God, a new creation. You have died with Him and been raised to a new life, a life of faith in Jesus.

3. Confess and turn away from any known sin and believe He removes your sin and remembers it no more. Receive the cleansing power of His blood.

4. Believe in the power of the blood of Jesus to make you holy and blameless in His sight. Give thanks and accept the grace and mercy that He freely gives.
   (Refuse to come to the Lord on any merit of your own. Good works, great prayers etc. are not the way to the Father – His blood is the only way we can enter His presence.)

✓ 5. Declare His victory over sin in your life. Sin no longer has dominion over you! You are made holy. Enjoy time with God receiving His love and acceptance.

Praying from heaven – seated in Christ

What I want to share with you now is a revelation that has the potential to radically reform your prayer life. When I caught this revelation of victory in my spirit I recognised that my prayers would never be the same again.

What I am talking about is the incredible spiritual position the Cross has placed us in. If we grasp the value of this position by faith our prayer life, thought life and attitude to the world around us will be completely different. We will see that we are in a position that can truly make a difference.

Jesus is in heaven

The Bible tells us that Jesus is no longer here in person. He has risen from the dead and is ascended and seated at the Father's right hand in heaven. The Holy Spirit, also called the Spirit of Christ, now brings the presence of Jesus into our hearts and lives.

> '...*He* [God] *raised Him from the dead and seated Him at His right hand in the heavenly places, far above all principality and power and might and dominion, and every name that is named, not only in this age but also in that which is to come.'*   (Ephesians 1:20–21)

Jesus is above every name and power, both in the physical world and in the spiritual world, the seen and unseen realms. The Son of God is seated in heaven and has finished His work for the needs and salvation of the world. Picture Him in this position of rest. He no longer has to do anything, but is waiting for everything to be put under His feet.

If He is there – where are you?

> *'For you died, and your life is hidden with Christ in God.'*
>   (Colossians 3:3)

Where Christ is, you are there too! Now the Bible clearly states that we were raised with Christ, and seated in heavenly places in Him.

> *'But God, who is rich in mercy, because of His great love with which He loved us, even when we were dead in trespasses, made us alive together with Christ (by grace you have been saved), and raised us up together, and made us sit together in the heavenly places in Christ Jesus . . . '*

(Ephesians 2:4–6)

You are seated in Christ in heavenly places!

This truth is not just for the future, for when we leave this earthly body and go to be with the Lord. It is true right now, as you sit and read this book. Your position 'in Christ' is far above every power and principality of darkness. You are seated with Him now in the greatest position of victory and success.

Every believer has been raised in Christ and is therefore in heavenly places. Let me remind you again, our work is to believe His Word.

So, what does this mean for me in my everyday life as a believer? How does this affect the way I think, act and pray? Well, if I am in Christ and He is in such an exalted position in heaven, then I am not confined or restricted to this earth and its powers. This means that when I pray, I can see myself already there in Christ in heavenly places, above all the problems and pressures of this world. I start to pray **from** my position of victory. I don't have to work my way **to** victory.

So whenever we pray let's remember that we are not trying to get to the throne of God. We are already there in heavenly places in Him, with heaven's provision available to us.

Of course we live out our lives here in our body, soul and spirit. We are human beings, and in our physical bodies we are earth-bound. But we are not like other people because our spirit is alive to God and we are with Him. We are called to live raised in Christ, with a very different perspective of life. This does not mean that we deny our needs and problems, but starting with a revelation of our position in heaven will create faith in our hearts for whatever miracle or provision we need.

See yourself with Christ in heaven right now, exalted and victorious in life.

Begin praying from heaven

Earlier, I used the example of a woman who told me that she felt like her prayers were bouncing off the ceiling. I'm sure we could all say that at times we don't experience or feel the nearness of God when we pray, but if we will believe our position in Christ, we will **know** where we are! No feeling or natural restriction will be able to hinder our prayer and communication with God.

Prayer begins with Jesus in heaven. Whenever a believer starts to pray with this truth in his heart and mind, he begins with victory in his spirit. His prayer and fellowship with God are not restricted by earthly things and he is **free** to be with God in heavenly places!

Many people begin to pray by focusing on the problem or need. **We must pray the answer and not the problem!** If we will ascend by faith to God's throne and see the provision there for every need, we will start to pray the answer. Please understand that this is God's Word and not a theory! He has given us this position in Christ so that we can glorify Him by living our lives in victory. A temptation we all face is to stay earth-bound with our focus on our problems. This has the effect of restricting our faith and reducing the effectiveness of our prayers. We must retrain ourselves to pray the answer. Let me give you an example of praying the answer:

'Lord, You are great and nothing is impossible for You. I come to You in faith that You will change my circumstances. Thank You for Your heart and will to bless me. I believe in Your power to provide for my every need. And so I thank You that You are doing great things on my behalf.'

Consider the flea!

I once heard an amazing fact about a flea. This little insect can jump incredibly high for its size – up to three feet! However, if you place a cover over one flea and restrict its jumping to three inches, then after a while remove the restriction, it will jump only as far as it has been trained or allowed – three inches! Yet, if you train it to jump to its full potential, then it will. This same behavioural pattern is evident with humans too! If we are restricted to perform at lower levels in prayer or in any area of life, then only that level will be reproduced through us. If we take off the restrictions and limitations of experience, opinion and anything else that limits us, then we will produce far more. For a believer, it's all a question of believing our position in Christ and behaving accordingly!

If we will rise up into the place we have in Jesus so that we can pray the way God wants us to pray, everything will change. As Jesus is far above **all**, so we are above all in Him. Everything Jesus has is ours, which includes all the victory over sin, death and hell.

> *'If then you were raised with Christ, seek those things which are above, where Christ is, sitting at the right hand of God. Set your mind on things above, not on things on the earth. For you died, and your life is hidden with Christ in God.'*
>
> (Colossians 3:1–3)

Setting our minds on things above brings us into line with God's will. In Christ we are in victory, joy, love, health and life! A believer doesn't try to be victorious – he is! The mistake many Christians make is that they are trying to get victory instead of accepting that Jesus has already given His victory to us. We begin with victory and continue in victory! We are above every circumstance and situation in Him.

Life can be full of trials and circumstances that wear us out and rob our faith. As soon as we are consumed more with the problems than the answers it's time to set our mind on Jesus and the victory. This is a crucial truth that has power to bring hope and faith into our hearts again. As soon as we return to faith in God, then we are on the path of victory!

Above all in Christ

You may have heard of some people who go to the top of high buildings and mountains to pray because they feel they have an advantage over the powers of darkness by doing so.

This of course is fine if the Lord asks you to do it – obedience will always bring victory. However, this 'natural' position does not change your position in Christ, you can't get a higher or greater one than that! It may help your mind gain perspective but there is no greater position than where you are in Christ – far above every name and power! Our faith is to rest in all that He has done for us on the Cross. He has given us everything – His life, His victory and power.

We need this to be **revelation** for our lives. If we live with this truth in our hearts and minds, we will rest in God's work and not struggle to attain what is already there for us. The Lord longs for us to believe Him and enter into the fullness of His riches and blessings. Trying to get the victory is not scriptural and will wear us out. Believing that in Christ we have the victory will bring peace into our hearts, even during the fiercest battle and trial, and give us faith to win. In truth we have everything that He has!

Watch what you think!

The key to living in this truth is to take hold of our minds and think in line with God's Word. This can be a difficult thing to do, but you are able to do this if you belong to Jesus. Jesus has set us free to think right. As we **set** our minds on things above by thinking about God's Word and His promises, we take captive every thought which contradicts truth and make it obedient to Christ. Faith will begin to rise in our heart and we will pray with heaven's perspective.

A few years ago I lived and worked for nearly a year in Washington DC. I was in a new country with unknown people and it was a great opportunity to develop my relationship with God! I spent hours in my bedroom praying, mainly because I had no-one else to talk to! God began to radically change my perspective during those times. As I prayed God began to show me the real needs of the city in visions. I saw individual people who were desperate for help – the addicts, murderers and broken lives. I prayed for the ones He showed me and was touched with His heart for them. As He opened my eyes to their needs, a question that was deep in my heart came to the surface. What could one person like me do to change what was happening to the people of this city? How could my prayer affect change in their lives? I can honestly say that I was not confident in prayer, nor did I consider myself an expert! I really felt overwhelmed by what God was showing me.

Then God flooded my heart with the answer. I could change **everything**! Because He has placed me in Christ and therefore above every need and power of darkness, I could believe God to change every situation I was seeing through **my** prayers. I was above all in Him so that I could pray His victory and life for them. Acting in His Name had little to do with me but everything to do with Him. With my mind on heaven's perspective, I was able to pray with faith and joy that God was bringing His will to the earth through me.

Application

1. Begin by thanking God that you are seated in Christ in heavenly places. Accept this as truth and ask the Holy Spirit to make this revelation for you.

2. Set your mind on Jesus and begin to speak to Him, declaring His goodness, grace and love. Let praise flow from your heart to Him and see yourself in Him in heavenly places.

3. Thank Him that you are above every demonic power and circumstance, in victory, peace and joy in Christ. Choose to believe the truth over and above everything. Hallelujah! As you see with His perspective, pray what you know He wants to do in and through your life.

Every time you pray – begin where you are – **in heavenly places in Christ**.

How to approach God's throne

The way we are to approach God in prayer is set out clearly for us in Scripture. There are many theories in the Church today about prayer and coming into His presence that are not based on God's Word. If we are to be successful in prayer we need to maintain a healthy respect for God and pray the way He has chosen for us to pray. God desires a loving and intimate relationship with every one of His children but we must always keep in mind **who** it is we are talking to! Acknowledging that we pray not only to a loving and merciful heavenly Father, but also to the One who is Lord and King, will produce a balanced and healthy attitude towards Him.

Right attitudes that bring blessing

A new respect and reverence for God is being restored to the Church. There is a growing understanding among God's people of His true character and nature. He is Holy **and** Father! This 'balanced' view changes the way we see God, and therefore, the way we relate to Him. We see many results in today's world of the breakdown of right attitudes to earthly authority. This promotes lack of respect for others and ultimately lawlessness. It's the same when we have a lack of respect for God. If believers have an unbalanced view of God it can produce wrong perspectives and, sometimes, wrong actions. As Christians, we are to know the blessings of being under God's authority and care. This is the safest place to be and brings true freedom and joy into our lives.

My own life with God has been greatly enriched through knowing Him not only as loving Father who wants to share His life and heart with me, but also as Awesome God before whom I willingly bow my whole being. Instead of making Him like another person in my thinking or even my equal, I recognise His greatness and this breeds the honour and respect for Him that He deserves. This, in turn, expands my faith in His power to change everything.

The Holy of Holies

In the light of all that Jesus has done on the Cross, we can look at the Old Testament scriptures to help us understand more about God's presence. Certain procedures were given by the Lord and were necessary to follow before man could approach Him.

After leaving Egypt, God chose to dwell among His people in a tabernacle or tent (see Exodus 26:1). Moses was given detailed instructions on how to make the tabernacle, but for our purposes in understanding how to approach God we will look at the general plan. There were three distinct sections or areas. They were called the outer court, the holy place and the Most Holy place, also called the Holy of Holies. The outer courts and holy place fulfilled certain functions and priests ministered there both day and night. However only one man, the high priest, could enter the Holy of Holies and this was just once a year. He came right through the holy place into the Most Holy place where God dwelt. Here he would make atonement for the sins of the people using the blood of animals.

This Most Holy place was honoured and revered by God's people, but it was also feared. The high priest would have a rope tied to his ankle so he could be dragged out if overcome by God's presence.

Today, our great High Priest Jesus has entered the Holy of Holies and with His blood sacrifice He has removed the veil that separated us from God. At the moment of Jesus' death the Temple curtain was torn in two – symbolic of the way He opened for us to come right into the Most Holy place. In Christ there is no longer anything that separates us from God, nor is there any restriction on the amount of time we can spend there with Him. Jesus has made this place open and available to every believer.

It is important to know that we are not to be afraid of entering His presence. He has shown us mercy and love. No longer do we need to stay in the outer courts – slightly removed from God. We can enter the Most Holy place by faith in Jesus and enjoy the most fulfilling relationship of our lives.

Come boldly

The **way** God wants us to approach Him is amazing when we recognise who it is we are meeting! Scripture tells us that God wants us to be **bold** when we approach Him. When we look back through the history of Israel and see how they related to God, we can only praise Him for the incredible grace we have been given in Jesus. Freedom to approach God and boldness before Him is a miracle of grace. Now, if someone is bold, they are courageous and confident in their attitude and actions. They don't hesitate or look like they are faltering. Understand that God does not want us to be timid and shy, but bold because we have been made worthy by His blood. True humility receives God's report and acts on it.

> *'Let us therefore come **boldly** to the throne of grace, that we may obtain mercy and find grace to help in time of need.'*
> (Hebrews 4:16)

We don't find judgement waiting for us, only mercy and grace to help us. We have the God-given right and commission to be with Him. We are not to behave as though we don't belong in His presence – He wants us to behave as His sons. We are welcome, accepted and loved by God and have been given a glorious inheritance in Christ. (Remember, in Christ there is neither male nor female – all are 'sons' and have the same right of inheritance – Galatians 3:28.)

> *'Therefore you are no longer a slave but a son, and if a son, then an heir of God through Christ.'*   (Galatians 4:7)

Receive all that is yours

Don't be apologetic about your inheritance and the position you have been given by God. Go in before His throne and receive it! Our heavenly Father loves us perfectly, has no favourites, and has given us a rich inheritance in Christ. It is so important for believers to find out what belongs to them, so that by faith (the way everything comes to us from God), we can receive all He has given. If I inherit a large sum of money from a relative, it would be of no use to me if I didn't know about it. Once I know the good news, then it's up to me to find out how to draw it out! It's the same with prayer. The blessings and provision that are ours need to be known and then drawn upon.

Knowing what belongs to us in Christ and drawing it out by faith pleases God. This boldness shows Him that you believe in the work of His Son. Your faith is in **Him** not **you**!

Let's look at another scripture that helps us to know how to approach God's throne:

> *'Therefore, brethren, having boldness to enter the Holiest by the blood of Jesus, by a new and living way which He consecrated for us, through the veil, that is, His flesh, and having a High Priest over the house of God, let us draw near with a true heart in full assurance of faith, having our hearts sprinkled from an evil conscience and our bodies washed with pure water.'* (Hebrews 10:19–22)

There are four 'keys' given in this scripture which, if applied, will help us to enter right into the presence of God:

1. We need to make the decision to come before God

We must decide to come before His throne. This is a very important point, although it seems obvious. It's amazing how apathy can keep us from making the decision to draw near to our Father. Positionally we are in Christ, but there needs to be a heart and mind choice to meet with Him. We draw near by faith to enter the throne room of heaven. As we **actively** draw near to Him, He promises to draw near to us (James 4:8). Once again, it's important to submit any feelings that deny the truth.

2. We are to be bold because of the blood

As I have mentioned before, being good and having a great prayer life does not qualify us – only the blood of Jesus gives us entry to the throne. Our performance or lack of it does not enable or disqualify us from meeting with God. Repentance and faith in Jesus is the way. We all start and finish with what Jesus has done. Recognising that in ourselves we have no right to be there requires sincere humility.

The throne room of heaven is where we are to be free from fear and free from the pressure to perform. In this place we are comfortable and 'at home'. Here we can receive and enjoy God's presence.

3. We are to come with a 'true' heart

A heart that is true is one that is **honest** with God. At times we can say things to God we don't mean, our lips speaking things we think God wants to hear but our heart is far away. We can go through the performance or ritual of prayer but in fact not meet with God at all. The Lord always knows what is really going on in our hearts. Be honest. Getting real with God makes all the difference in prayer! Psalm 62:8 tells us to pour out our hearts to Him – this is where true prayer really begins. He wants us to be real with Him and to be speaking from our hearts. However, be careful not to focus on yourself, but make Jesus the centre of your prayers.

Note: Often as we begin to pray our words can seem distant and empty – as though we don't mean what we are saying. Our hearts appear to be cold and disinterested even though we really do intend to draw near to God. This is where we can feel condemned if we are not careful. If this happens don't fall into the devil's trap and think that you are being a hypocrite. Keep going and tell the Lord you genuinely want to meet with Him and receive from Him even though you have no strong feelings as you pray. Perseverance will reap rewards as you determine to be real with the Lord and share your heart with Him. You will find that after a while you will come through to a new place of genuine, heart-felt prayer if you keep on going. Don't give up but encourage yourself to enter right into His presence.

4. We are to have full assurance of faith
Faith is being sure and certain of the things we don't see or necessarily feel (Hebrews 11:1). We please God when we believe that He is, and that He rewards those who diligently seek Him (Hebrews 11:6). **Faith has rewards!** As we believe that we are before the throne, God is pleased and will reward us. Unbelief keeps us out of God's presence and promises. Faith releases God's presence and promises into our lives. We will receive full assurance and confidence as we begin to walk by faith and not by sight.

Application
1. Praise Him for the joy of knowing that the veil has been torn in two and nothing separates you from God. You can now enter right into the Most Holy place and be with Him.

2. Make a decision to approach God's throne now.

3. Be reverent but come boldly and confidently as a son of God, fully accepted in His sight. As you approach Him, thank Him for His love and mercy to receive you. Pour out in you own words your desire to be with Him and meet with Him. Be genuine in your heart and keep your mind on Him.

4. Believe that you are there before the eternal throne of God and thank Him for the amazing grace that enables us to be in this place. Enjoy His presence. Give Him worship and praise and be free to spend some time receiving. (Remember that you need to continue to believe as you receive. It's not what you feel, but what you believe that is important.)

Chapter 3

Knowing the Lord

Having established the foundational truths that put us in the right position for prayer, we can now move on to talk about relationship. I once read somewhere a simple comment that helps me to remain focused on God's priorities for my life:

'Keep the main thing the main thing.'

The main thing isn't productivity or what we 'achieve' in prayer – it's relationship. The first and greatest commandment the Lord gave was that we should love Him with all our heart, mind, soul and strength. This helps us to see that we are not prayer 'machines' that just do a job to produce results, but we are people who are primarily called to love.

Your relationship with Him

' . . . for in Him we live and move and have our being.'
(Acts 17:28)

A few years ago, a friend and I went on mission to Burundi and Rwanda in Central Africa. Some of you may remember the trauma these two countries endured during the genocide of 1994. We were privileged to meet various people there whose faith has since had such an impact on our lives. Most of them were locals, although we did meet a well-seasoned American missionary of 83. He knew the Lord well and was a real inspiration, not least because he had 5000 refugees living in his back garden! His life demonstrated the gospel at work and it was a great privilege to meet him and his wife and see the service they were providing to support and care for these people. I will always remember his comment to me as we left:

> 'Judith, whether you are from Africa or America, East or West, always tell people that strength and success in life come from knowing God personally and spending time in the secret place.'

What a friend we have in Jesus

Jesus is **the** most dependable friend we can ever have. He never fails to love us and believe the best for us, even when we doubt ourselves. Knowing Him brings a deep stability, strength and satisfaction into our lives. Everything else may change but He remains the same. If we develop a strong and vital relationship with Him we will see His blessing and provision released into our lives.

Note:

I would just like to add that some people get confused about who to pray to – the Father, Jesus or the Holy Spirit. He is One God, and so there really is freedom to use whichever Name is on your heart. Jesus said to pray to the Father in His Name, receiving help from the Holy Spirit as your Comforter and Helper. Don't let this be a point of confusion or distraction as He is One. If you prefer to talk to Jesus or the Father, be free. I sometimes will address all Three in my prayers.

People who **know** God will do great things. As a result, we will find ourselves doing things that surpass our natural abilities. All fruitfulness comes from living in Him and knowing Him. When our prayer lives are weak, we are not able to walk as Jesus intends. We lack joy and peace and have little vision and faith. On the other hand, when we are strong in our relationship with Him, we can believe all things and have great vision for our lives. We will experience joy and peace with God's power being released continuously in and through us.

'I have come that they may have life, and that they may have it more abundantly.' (John 10:10)

The word 'revival' actually means to come back to life. Jesus has given us fullness of life as a gift, so we already have the potential as believers to live in His fullness. However, for various reasons, we are not yet living in all that we have been given.

What is the scriptural answer for us as we seek to live as Jesus intends? If we are to experience revival – a coming back to life as God desires – we need to live a life of faith in God's Word with total dependency on the Holy Spirit, constantly yielding our hearts and minds to His way and not our own.

Heart or head communication

How we communicate with God is important. Long prayers of fine sounding words will not necessarily bring fellowship with God. For those of us who don't feel that our words in prayer are eloquent and flow easily, this is good news. The prayer that comes from the heart and not just the head is the kind of prayer God responds to.

Many times I have been praying with a group of believers, and the moment when one of them opens their heart and prays a genuine prayer to God is the moment I know we have what we are asking for. The ones with all the right ways of saying things, who pray to please man and not God, already have their reward (Matthew 6:5).

Heart involvement is the main issue during communion with the Lord. Yes, we have been given minds to use for God's purposes and our minds are important, but a revival relationship with Him starts from the heart. The Bible calls the heart the centre or 'spirit' of a man.

'For thus says the High and Lofty One who inhabits eternity, whose name is Holy: I dwell in the high and holy place, with him who has a contrite [repentant] *and humble spirit, to revive the spirit of the humble, and to revive the heart of the contrite ones.'* (Isaiah 57:15)

A humble and repentant heart is the kind that God promises to revive. What does this mean? Well, essentially this is a heart that is willing to be corrected and changed. This does not mean that we go on a constant self-analysis trip to discover our faults. If we do this, we would be overwhelmed by our own failures. However, if our hearts are humble, we will acknowledge that we are not yet living a perfect life and allow the Holy Spirit to show us where change is needed. Then, we can repent and rely on Him to help us to change. The key is to allow God to work the change in us and not try to change ourselves – **impossible**!

The apostle Paul considered everything else worthless in comparison to the greatness of knowing Jesus. We are to pursue the knowledge of Jesus with all that we are, totally abandoned to Him and dedicated to fulfilling His purposes in our lives. Coming to Jesus with a heart that is open and willing to receive the mercy and grace He offers will bring His reviving touch.

Revival is God's intention and best for every believer. So the question is, how can we experience and live in this revival?

Two different ways to be with Jesus

There is a chapter in Luke's gospel that highlights some radical differences between heart and head communication with Jesus. Let's take a look at Luke 7:36–50:

The story begins with Simon, who was a Pharisee and probably quite important in Jewish society. Having heard about Jesus, he was interested to find out more, and so he invited Him around for a meal.

During this meal a woman who was a renowned sinner burst in uninvited and almost 'threw herself' at Jesus. Imagine the impact she made on the party. The kind of people who were there would never associate with her under normal circumstances. She was carrying a jar of expensive fragrant oil and proceeded to pay special attention to Jesus. She kissed His feet and cried so much that she had to wipe the tears away with her hair. She broke open the jar and poured out the oil onto His feet.

Imagine yourself there, witnessing this display of extra-vagant emotion and love. Rather embarrassing for the onlookers! I don't suppose they really knew how to react or what to do.

We must keep in mind that God, the Holy One, is in this house. Here are two people relating to Him in very different ways. Simon wants to genuinely find out **about** Jesus. He is watching and assessing the way Jesus responds to the woman. The woman on the other hand doesn't see anybody else but Jesus. She is not interested in Simon's reaction and probably doesn't even notice him. Man had rejected her most of her life but she saw something in this Person that compelled her. She was drawn to Him, this Rabbi and Miracle Worker. (May it never cease to amaze us that the 'Sinless One' draws sinners to Himself.) His love was so powerful and real to her that she was prepared to break every social and religious barrier to reach Him. Even her own fears and shame couldn't stop her. She knew somehow that He would receive her and accept her. Fear of man's opinion and her own sin, failure and low self-esteem would not stop her either. She was determined.

She demonstrated to Jesus her genuine, heart-felt repent-ance and as she humbled herself before Him, she was overcome by His unspoken acceptance. In all this she was acknowledging her need for Him.

Simon, standing at a distance, watching the scene, contin-ued to assess Jesus. His relationship was mind-centred and based on observation and interest. The woman on the other hand was most definitely responding to Jesus with her heart.

Now we know this scripture speaks to us about the saving power of God's love and His willingness to accept sinners. However, we can learn a lot about prayer from this passage. There is a stark contrast between these two relationships.

What does God want from us?

Firstly, we must understand that God has no favourites, we are all of equal value to Him. He loves Simon just as much as He loves the woman. Simon also needs to receive forgiveness for his sins but he does not acknowledge this. To him, Jesus is an unusual man, travelling around Israel, saying and doing some extraordinary things that have captured his interest. But as yet, there is no humbling in Simon's heart to recognise Jesus. This is the main point of difference between the two people. One knows without doubt, Jesus is her only hope. The other is still assessing and making his judgements.

Jesus turns to the woman and begins to address Simon:

> *'Do you see this woman? I entered your house; you gave Me no water for My feet, but she has washed My feet with her tears and wiped them with the hair of her head. You gave Me no kiss, but this woman has not ceased to kiss My feet since the time I came in. You did not anoint My head with oil, but this woman has anointed My feet with fragrant oil. Therefore, I say to you, her sins, which are many, are forgiven, for she loved much. But to whom little is forgiven, the same loves little.'* (Luke 7:44–47)

He talks about this excessive display of emotion and affection as though it were of real value to Him. He received her love, affection and tears. Jesus is actually showing Simon that he has missed the secret to receiving from God – *giving*.

God's love is indescribable and extravagant, demonstrated to us through Jesus dying for us. He is not measuring out small doses of love at certain intervals, when we've been good or are doing well in our walk with Him. He loves us every minute of every day with unconditional, powerful love. Because He loves us, He wants us to love Him **extravagantly**. And, amazingly He's put the resources within us to do it – the Holy Spirit.

This woman demonstrated her love for Jesus by giving everything she was and had! She brought treasure with her and gave Him her best. Even though her heart was broken, full of sin and shame, Jesus restored her with His mercy and acceptance, and she left changed, convinced of His love for her.

Simon sat and talked with Jesus but didn't give himself to Jesus. He had no comprehension of the mercy he needed or the value of the intimate relationship he had missed with Him.

The woman's desperation brought God's power into her life. She left forgiven, healed, restored and **full** of Jesus. Simon was left probably a little challenged, but ultimately not changed!

We must meet Jesus with our whole being and not just our minds

---

Prayer must progress from the mind to the heart if we are to really encounter God and receive from Him. I believe there can be traces of 'Simon' in all of us at times. We invite Jesus into our lives to be our Lord and genuinely want to know Him but our minds can dominate and be a stumbling block. This restricts our faith and keeps us away from the joy of heart to heart communication with our Lord.

Jesus shows us here from His Word that the issue we must face is recognising our need for Him. A holy desperation for Jesus will bring revival in our relationship with Him. He will impact us with His life as we humbly approach Him with desire for Him alone.

Loving Jesus

Our prayer times need to be full of loving Jesus. Loving Him with all that we are and have will bring great blessing. Notice the scripture says that since the time Jesus came in this woman had not stopped kissing Him. Another definition for worship is to 'kiss'! Since the time Jesus came into our hearts have we stopped worshipping Him and loving Him? Man may be embarrassed at this open display of love, but God isn't. Our first ministry or call as believers is to love the Lord and worship Him. Out of this **abandonment** to Him we are able to meet with Him, touch His heart and receive all He wants to give.

Head or mind prayers will never get you into this place of intimacy with God. Coming to Him in sincerity of heart, longing to give and receive, will bring Jesus into every area of life. Yes, we are saved. But we must go on to know Jesus, meeting daily with Him in His mercy, love and grace. This brings a fresh revelation to us of Jesus and the joy of our salvation. God always sees and looks at our hearts. We must push through every barrier to get to Jesus and worship Him. He has broken down every wall of separation for us to be with Him.

When we come to Jesus and we see how much we have been forgiven, thanksgiving will certainly pour from our hearts. A new fire of love for Him begins.

How inexpressible is the gift He has given to us in Christ. Just talking from our mind, without engaging our heart, robs us of the sweet communion that is available for every believer. When we have this daily heart fellowship with our Lord, His glory will fill and be seen in our lives.

Others will see that we have been with Jesus

I remember talking with a pastor from Burundi (Africa) about his father, who was a minister during the East African revival. As a young boy, rather than go off and play with his friends, he would wait outside the room when his father was praying. The reason for waiting was the reward of seeing his father's face which would shine with the glory of God. Isn't it incredible that this was so attractive to this three- or four-year-old boy? I later learned the believers in this revival were called 'the shining ones' as their faces actually shone with the presence of God.

> *'But we all, with unveiled face, beholding as in a mirror the glory of the Lord, are being transformed into the same image from glory to glory, just as by the Spirit of the Lord.'*
>
> (2 Corinthians 3:18)

Application

1. Ask the Lord to help you break though any barriers you may have to being open-hearted with Him.

2. Decide to submit your own thoughts and talk to Jesus from your heart.

3. Present and surrender everything you are and have to Him. Abandon yourself to Him. Humble yourself before Him and tell Him He is everything you need. Turn away from your own ways and be changed into His image.

4. Ask the Holy Spirit to help you to pour out your love and worship at His feet. Minister to Jesus with thanksgiving and adoration for all that He is and has done for you. Really give yourself to Him and worship. Go further than you have been with Him before. Be free to weep or rejoice! Let Him minister His love and healing, life and strength to your heart.

5. Receive from Him by faith.

The importance of worship in prayer

We see from reading the Gospels that people would often worship Jesus before they asked Him for help. This was the first and most 'natural' response that brought the right heart of submission and honour for the Lord.

> *'And behold, there came a man named Jairus, and he was a ruler of the synagogue. And he fell down at Jesus' feet and begged Him to come to his house, for he had an only daughter about twelve years of age, and she was dying.'*
> (Luke 8:41–42)

This man was desperate for a miracle. He didn't just ask Jesus to come and see his daughter, he actually fell at His feet acknowledging that the One he came to was worthy of honour, respect and worship. From this humble position he asks the Master for help. Prayer flows sweetly from a heart of submission and worship. No matter how desperate we are, Jesus is always worthy of our worship and praise. Worship prepares our hearts to pray and receive miracles from God.

Prayer and worship are inseparable as both bring us into relationship with God. I like to say they are 'married'! As with prayer, worship also takes place before God's throne. The importance of worship is shown in Jesus' teaching on prayer. He actually teaches us to begin prayer with worship.

> *'So He said to them, when you pray, say: Our Father in heaven, hallowed be Your name.'* (Luke 11:2)

To hallow God means to give Him honour. When we 'hallow' His name we praise and worship Him for His holiness, power, majesty and glory. He is Awesome, Father, Wonderful, Mighty etc. Names are very important in Scripture as they describe character. There are many names for God in the Bible that reveal His character and ways to us. We are to use them in our worship to expand our revelation of who He is and give Him the honour He is due.

The anointing of the Holy One

We have been given an anointing from God that enables us to pray and worship (1 John 2:20). Within every believer's heart there is a well of life – God's Spirit – who anoints us and gives life to our worship. Our hearts become open and yielded before God as we worship, ready to be directed according to His will.

> *'The king's heart is in the hand of the Lord, like the rivers of water; He turns it wherever He wishes.'*   (Proverbs 21:1)

If we find that our heart is cold or hard, true worship will restore the softness and fire. We then change to prefer His prayer agenda and not our own. As oil enables an engine to work, so the Holy Spirit anoints us to worship and we can flow with such ease from worship into prayer. We don't have to stop and think about what to pray when we have begun with worship – we are led easily into the prayers of the Spirit.

There really is a great difference in the way I pray if I have spent time in worship first. When I am on my own with God I know that if I truly worship Him first then I will pray very differently. Why? Well, my focus changes from self or circumstances to Jesus. My heart becomes softer and more loving with God's compassion filling my prayers.

To worship Him in the beauty of His Holiness will fill us with awe. Selfish desires will fade away and His will and desire will fill our heart.

Take time

There is always a temptation to rush our time with the Lord and pray about everything and everyone on our minds. We forget just to love and minister to Him. One of the reasons for dull and lifeless praying is a lack of time spent in worship. If we take time to worship Him first, our prayers will be fresh and full of life. (For more details on spending time with God see the next section 'Alone with God in the secret place.')

Ministering to the Lord is a priority for believers and enables Spirit-filled and Spirit-led prayer. As we worship, we see Him with the eyes of faith, high and lifted up, seated on the throne. He is surrounded by the hosts of heaven who are constantly giving Him glory, honour and praise. As you are reading this all heaven is worshipping the risen, glorified Lamb who was slain for the sins of the world. There is praise and adoration, loud voices declaring His glory with elders and angels falling down before Him. Heaven never rests in its worship of God.

> *'Then I looked, and I heard the voice of many angels around the throne, the living creatures, and the elders; and the number of them was ten thousand times ten thousand, and thousands of thousands, saying with a loud voice: "Worthy is the Lamb who was slain to receive power and riches and wisdom, and strength and honour and glory and blessing!"'*
> (Revelation 5:11–12)

Our worship joins in with the constant worship of heaven

We are to join in with this constant worship and give to Jesus the glory, honour, thanksgiving and praise. There is a principle for worship that is set in heaven – to **give**. To worship God takes time and a certain amount of effort. Our self-life (or flesh) does not like the sacrifice that worship requires. Worship is for God **not** ourselves, although we reap far more from His presence than we give.

We are unable to enter into true worship by being self-centred. Our worship must centre on God and not on ourselves. There are times for singing about who we are in Christ, and proclaiming all that He has done for us. But worship is all **about Him** and is just **for Him**.

Worship in spirit and in truth

Jesus said the Father is looking for true worshippers:

> *'But the hour is coming, and now is, when the true*
> *worshippers will worship the Father in spirit and truth; for*
> *the Father is seeking such to worship Him.'*   (John 4:23)

The Bible tells us that God is Spirit and we must worship Him in spirit (John 4:24). Man is made up of three parts – spirit, soul and body. The spirit is the heart or centre of a man, the soul consists of mind, will and emotions, and the body is the vessel we live in here on earth. Our spirit man is of great importance to God when it comes to worship and prayer. To Him we **are** spirit, we **have** a soul and we **live** in a body! The Holy Spirit dwells in our spirit (or inner man). God's river of life flows from our inner man, through our souls and out of our bodies.

Jesus said:

> *'He who believes in Me, as the scripture has said, out of his*
> *heart* [or inner man] *will flow rivers of living water. But this*
> *He spoke concerning the Spirit, whom those believing in Him*
> *would receive; for the Holy Spirit was not yet given, because*
> *Jesus was not yet glorified.'*   (John 7:38–39)

Whenever we worship God, His Spirit anoints us and leads us to worship. As we worship, God's river of life flows through our body and soul and we express our love and praise to Him.

The Holy Spirit is our worship leader and the One who enables and empowers us to worship. We must be filled with Him as He is our **Helper** in worship. God is not contacted with our body or even our soul. He is Spirit. Like communes with like – spirit with Spirit. Yes – the Bible tells us to use our body and soul in worship – hands, voice, mind, emotions etc., but we meet with Him through our spirit and receive from Him through our spirit.

Word-filled worship is worship in truth, so our songs and words need to be full of God's Word. Jesus called the Holy

Spirit the Spirit of Truth. When our worship is Spirit-filled and led, it will be full of the truth, full of the Word and therefore full of Jesus. Whenever you give worship to God, the Holy Spirit will be working within you to bring you fresh revelation of Jesus. The more we see Him, the more we love and respond to Him. This creates new vision and a fresh desire to worship. One other important aspect of worship in truth is that our hearts are to be genuinely engaged as we worship.

Note:

Songs and music are a vehicle to express what is in our hearts to God. The Book of Psalms often encourages us to sing a new song to the Lord. This may come in the form of an old song, but because it expresses our heart to the Lord – it's a new song! Singing using the gift of tongues, the spiritual language God gives us, will also bring our spirit into communication with God. Whether the words you are using are understandable to you or not, speak or sing them out in faith.

Application

1. Be filled with the Holy Spirit (Ephesians 5:18). This is not a one-time event, but should be a regular request. How are we filled? By asking the Lord. The way to receive is to ask and believe that you have received (Luke 11:13). Remember not to measure your receiving by what you feel. We receive by faith.

2. Choose to worship God. Present your spirit, soul and body to Him and set your mind on Jesus. Shut out every other influence and focus on Him. (It often helps to close your eyes.)

3. Begin to speak out your love and praise to Him. Enter into His courts with thanksgiving and praise (Psalm 100:4). Let the vision of Jesus, risen and glorified fill your mind and heart, see with the eyes of faith that you are joining with heaven's worship of the King of kings. Let the river of praise pour from your heart and out of your mouth.

4. The Holy Spirit will bring to your remembrance the truth as you worship, e.g. 'You are altogether lovely Jesus, full of grace and truth.' 'You are majestic in Holiness.' 'Holy and awesome is Your Name.' All these words are from Scripture. Let the Spirit give you words as you worship. Expect to see Him with the eyes of faith.

   Poets are very elaborate and expansive in their description of the most simple things. They can even make the most ordinary object sound interesting and desirable with their words. We are worshipping Jesus whose character and beauty far surpasses anything in all creation. We also have the Creative One living in us to help us worship. Our words and vocabulary should be full of revelation of His unending glory, His Holiness and majesty.

5. Sing to Him a new song! Sing songs you know and those unknown but inspired and given by the Spirit to you as you worship. New songs are to fill our hearts. Every one of us can sing a new song to the Lord. So, with the Holy Spirit, create new songs as you worship. These songs are for Him, and He loves your voice (even if others don't!) We can soon run out of words to express our love and worship. God has given us a heavenly language to worship and sing to Him with – be free to use it.

Note:
One way that will help you worship God is to take a Psalm and speak it aloud or even sing it to your own tune. Try this with Psalm 96. Personalise the words – e.g. I will sing a new song, I proclaim the good news of grace, of your love and kindness etc. Develop this by choosing your own psalms or scriptures or even write your own psalm.

Alone with God in the secret place

'But you, when you pray, go into your room, and when you have shut your door, pray to your Father who is in the secret place; and your Father who sees in secret will reward you openly.' (Matthew 6:6)

There is no alternative and no other way – we all must have time on our own with God. The devil will try to make our lives so busy and our flesh will prefer other activities or company, but it is essential for us to have time alone with God. **Without personal time with Him we are weak, our love for Him fails and we become worldly!** The influence of other things will crowd out the holy influence of God if we allow them to.

The more we have to do in life, the more we need God's wisdom and power to help us. Prayer and communion with God will prepare us for the things God has for us to do every day and will alert us to the distractions of the flesh and the devil. Now, this holds different challenges for each one of us. The circumstances of our lives will vary so much – one may have small children, another may run a business or work long hours, and yet another may have hours to spare each day. But, for all of us the words of Jesus are the same. It's not 'if' but 'when' you pray.

No-one else can develop your personal time with God. Each one of us chooses to make time for God. Excuses can always be made, and I have made some wonderful ones in my time, but we need to just do it!

Finding time to pray

Many believers are stretched and pushed to their limits with work, family and church commitments. Time with God can quickly become last on the list of priorities, not first! Having no or very little effective time with God is a deceptive trap we can easily fall into – 'I just haven't had time to pray today.' Even if our lives are busy, our priority every day should be to spend time with God. Jesus spoke about a man having worked all day who came home and served his master first before he himself sat down for something to eat! (Luke 17:7–10). This is a challenging word, but we need to see beyond the sacrifice to the joy that awaits us. When time with God is a priority, God's order comes into our life. If we sow time with God we will reap rewards. Our life will be ordered by Him, and filled with peace, wisdom and purpose.

The truth about prayer is our flesh is weak – but the spirit is **willing.** If we learn not to give in to our own fleshly desires, we will discover a willingness to pray that comes from within. The key is to take the first step and go into the room to be alone with Him.

In all the years I have walked with the Lord, I can honestly say that the biggest influence in my life and the place where I have been changed most is the prayer closet. The Holy Spirit will draw us, not push us into prayer. So our flesh may complain a little – but we have a choice. Once we get there, we have won a great victory over self and can expect to receive rewards from God as we pray. Making this decision will go a long way to living a joy-filled relationship with God.

Prayer brings the power of God into life. When our lives are saturated with prayer, we will live with the supernatural provision of God and live to see everything and everyone changing around us.

Training for life

A life of prayer doesn't just fall on us. It is something we develop by spending time with God. Just as a marriage or any relationship needs time and commitment to develop and grow, so does our relationship with God. The Christian life is a process of growth to maturity in Christ. It's up to us to train and discipline ourselves to be alone in His presence.

Growing up

This may not be your experience at all, but when I was first born-again it was so easy for me to spend time with God. I was overwhelmed by God's loving acceptance and I really did seem to experience a 'honeymoon' period. After a while I found that my **feelings** changed, and prayer began to become a walk of pure faith. I actually wondered if I had backslidden, but after a while I realised that God was developing my faith. This was a hard lesson to learn, to simply believe. I knew that God had not changed, even if I didn't feel anything, He was the same loving Father I had experienced before.

During the next season, the Lord began to show me areas in my life that did not please Him – sin that I was living with that I hadn't seen or acknowledged before. I learned to confess my sin to Him, repent and believe in His forgiveness. (Of course, this is an ongoing process.)

After some time of 'introspection', the Lord revealed to me that the purpose of the secret place was to meet with Him and to pray – not just to get my life right with Him. Spending all my time in repentance was not what He required and was robbing our fellowship together. I needed to progress into intimacy with Him and then into prayer for others. Here He would minister to me and show me who to pray for and what to pray. My prayers became led by Him.

Now, each one of us should be able to look back and see the changes and developments in our relationship with God. We must always be moving forward with Him, willing and open to change. Then our relationship will grow in depth and love as we pursue knowledge and intimacy with Him. Let Jesus lead you as you enter through the new and living way (Hebrews 10:20).

You are a house of prayer

> *'Even them I will bring to My Holy mountain, and make them joyful in My house of prayer. Their burnt offerings and their sacrifices will be accepted on My altar; for My house shall be called a house of prayer for all nations.'*

> (Isaiah 56:7)

Do you believe what you have just read, that God will make you **joyful** in prayer? The Bible says that in His presence is fullness of joy. So, of course there should be joy in prayer. Even if we see people in great need there is always joy in God's presence for us to receive as we carry their needs to the Father. Nothing is too difficult for God and He will answer us. Believing God releases His joy.

We are called the temple of the Holy Spirit, the 'house' or dwelling place of God (1 Corinthians 6:19). No longer does God reside in a tent or temple building as He did in Old Testament times. Now, He lives in believers. God calls us His house of prayer and we are called to pray for all nations. There is no limit, restriction or distance in the Spirit, our prayers can go anywhere, all over the world. If I pray for China tonight then they will receive the blessing of

God. Our prayers can touch any person in the world at any time.

We need to understand that every believer has a ministry of prayer and not just those with a recognised 'gift' for intercession. We all have a God-given responsibility to pray for our families, friends, neighbours, nation, etc. – being a house of prayer means that God's power through you is reaching those far and near.

I read a testimony about Jackie Pullinger, an English missionary working in the Walled City, Hong Kong. She once told of spending three days alone in her room praying. The Lord led her in prayer for all those who never had anyone pray for them. She wept as the heart of God touched her heart with the spiritual, physical and emotional needs of the people. I'm convinced that each one of us can trace our salvation back to someone who prayed for us. In reality, you may be the only person who has ever prayed for your neighbour or the person who sits next to you on the train. Quite a sobering thought!

God gives and increases our desire for prayer

It really is true to say that the more you pray, the more you will want to pray. If I am going through a particularly difficult time and am finding it hard to pray I will ask Him to help and give me renewed desire. I don't wait for a feeling, but I act on it and believe He has answered me. There will be a fresh release of grace to pray.

> *'For he who sows to his flesh will of the flesh reap corruption, but he who sows to the Spirit will of the Spirit reap ever-lasting life.'*   (Galatians 6:8)

We reap what we sow. Giving time to fleshly things will produce fleshly living. Giving time to the things of God will produce godly living. For example, watching too much television will increase the desire for more. We can quickly get into the wrong habits that feed our selfish desires. Reading the Word and prayer will increase the desire for God and His Kingdom. You will reap either flesh or Spirit depending on where you are sowing. A farmer knows he will not have a harvest if he doesn't first spend time sowing the seed. You get a harvest in prayer from where you have sown, and you will in due season reap the results (Galatians 6:9).

> **The secret place transforms you,**
> **moulds you and prepares you**
> **to walk with God through the day!**

Application

1. Make a specific time each day to be alone with God. Jesus often went to pray in the early morning. This really is the best time as there is no-one better to start the day with. Getting out of bed is a discipline, but once you have developed a lifestyle of early-morning prayer it becomes easier. (Of course, other times during the day are good, but starting with Jesus is best!)

2. Go into your room and shut the door. Find a room or place where you can be alone with no distractions. Shut the door on the world and all its problems and shut out the lying, accusing voice of the devil. Be alone with God. (Always take your Bible with you – it's your prayer manual.) Meet with Him, worship, read the Word and let Him speak to you.

3. Pray to your Father who is in the secret place. Don't just **think** about praying – pray. Thinking is not prayer. Be a house of prayer, and let the Lord lead you to pray for whoever is on **His** heart.

4. He sees in secret and will reward you openly. He will reward this time. Others will see these rewards in you and through your life. You will change. Praying people get results in answered prayer, they have an understanding of the will and heart of God, they are full of vision, faith and power. They are continuously being refreshed from the presence of the Lord.

Some further advice

If you are not used to spending time with God, don't begin
by setting impossible targets. Start with 10–15 minutes a day
and build from there. Vary what you do and don't get stuck
on methods or ways to meet with God. Be with God with
your heart. Sing, pray in tongues, worship, praise, give
thanks, read the Word, listen, sit, lie. (Don't get too comfortable or you may fall asleep.) Walk or even jump around etc.
What works for one person won't always work for another.
Also, what works on one occasion might not be appropriate
for another. Allow the Holy Spirit to lead you.

Finally, if you have an extremely busy life, ask God to help
you change or rearrange something so that you can pray. Be
aware that Satan will try to put other things in your way to
prevent you from praying – resist him and determine to be in
the secret place every day. You will reap enormous benefits.

Hearing His voice

Success in the Christian life is found in our ability to hear
God's voice and act on what we hear. The importance of
hearing Him will, at times, have awesome consequences.
Recently I was told of a lady missionary who was presented
with an incredible opportunity whilst ministering in India.
She looked across the sea and saw a tiny island in the
distance. Turning to the pastor she asked, 'Has anyone ever
carried out an evangelistic mission on that island?' She was
responding to the voice of the Holy Spirit stirring her heart.
The pastor had never known of anyone who had, and so
together they planned a mission for the next time she was
there. The island had about 5000 inhabitants and almost
3000 of them responded and gave their lives to Jesus. Some
time later the missionary returned, hoping to help the new
church which had been set up. To her shock and amazement
she discovered that the entire island had been destroyed by
a 'freak' storm. Not one person had survived! God could
foresee all that was going to happen and in His love and
mercy had a plan for their eternal salvation. He needed
someone to listen to His voice and respond. A very sobering
and yet motivational testimony. She was hearing His voice

and walking in obedience that brought life to others. We are God's ambassadors here on earth, representing Him and speaking the Word He gives us.

God wants to speak to us regularly and give His direction and will in everything. If we will incline our ear to hear, we will have His success in life.

> *'My sheep hear My voice, and I know them, and they follow Me.'* (John 10:27)

The first step to hearing God is believing you can

We are equipped to hear His voice. Did you know that sheep have the ability to recognise their own shepherd's voice from other voices? In Israel there are occasions when three or four different flocks may gather together to drink at the same place. When this happens they intermingle and become one large flock. To us this may appear to be an administrative nightmare! However, when the shepherds begin to walk away in their different directions calling their sheep as they go, they separate and move back into their original group. Each sheep knows and follows their own shepherd's voice. Isn't that amazing? In the same way, every believer has been designed by God to recognise His voice and follow Him. God is a communicator and has many things He wants to say to each one of us.

Too many Christians agree with the 'father of lies', the devil, who tells them that they can't hear God. They walk around confessing this enemy-inspired lie. This lie can hinder our relationship with God if we believe it. **Never agree with a lie – only agree with the truth**. Be careful what you speak out as your words have power to bring death or life. If you confess you can't hear God, then you won't! (Proverbs 18:21). Agree with the truth that you are designed by God to hear Him and follow where He leads. He is your Good Shepherd.

Of course, as part of the body of Christ we are wise to ask advice from godly leaders and from those who are more mature in the faith than we are. This is especially important if we are making major decisions in life. However, we are to grow in our own ability to hear God so that we can mature in our relationship with Him. Don't depend on others to hear God for you but allow others to confirm or even at times disagree with what you believe you are hearing. This is God's 'safety net' to prevent us from making wrong decisions. Now, along with everyone else, I have made my mistakes and thought I'd heard God when I hadn't! This failure should not put us off. We must encourage ourselves that we are developing and growing in the knowledge of Him and His will.

We find that the more familiar we are with a person, the more we are able to recognise their voice. If a particular friend calls me on the 'phone I will know who it is a soon as he or she speaks. The more we progress in our knowledge of God, the more we will recognise Him when He speaks. Using another illustration about sheep, one of the fundamental differences between sheep and lambs is that lambs will follow the other sheep and not the shepherd. The mature sheep will know and follow the shepherd. Immature Christians do hear God but need more support and help as they grow and develop to recognise God's voice clearly for themselves.

Learning to listen to Him

Every relationship needs two-way communication for it to prosper and grow. Friendships happen and grow through communication and understanding. Friends are not friends if there is no understanding or knowledge about one another. If it's a one way relationship, then it's not true friendship. It is no different when it comes to a believer's relationship with God. Incessant talking to God with no real listening makes it a one way relationship. Most of us find being quiet and listening a difficult thing and we need to train ourselves to do it. I'm sure we have all realised that what God has to say to us is far more important than what we are usually planning to say to Him. One Word from God has power to change everything.

Whose voice are you hearing?

There are many different voices that compete for our attention. There is our own voice, which we hear most of our waking lives as we speak silently within ourselves. There is also the voice of the enemy that can invade our minds with suggestions and lies, criticisms and accusations. Then there are our friends and families opinions together with many other voices that come through television, video, radio and music etc. Finally and most importantly, there is the voice of the Lord. If we listen and place what He says over and above every other word, there will be peace and success for us. The world, the flesh and the devil can succeed in crowding out God's voice to us, but only if we allow it.

The different ways God speaks

The big question is – how do we know when it's God speaking?

Well, He speaks to us in a variety of ways. Perhaps the most important thing for you and me to know is that He will not contradict His Word; everything He says will always be in line with Scripture. Another good test to check that we are hearing God is to identify whether or not we have peace in our hearts. Now, let me qualify this. When God speaks our flesh may not like it because flesh opposes the Spirit (Galatians 5:17). But our inner man will rejoice and we will have a deep sense of peace and calm in our spirit. Let me illustrate this point by sharing a personal testimony.

About three years ago just before going to sleep one night I heard God speak quietly into my heart. What I heard was something I'd never considered before. He told me that I was to go into the local hospice and do some voluntary work. I must tell you that I have a natural aversion to hospitals and particularly hospices. I nursed my mother who died of cancer many years before and had once vowed to a friend that I would never go into a hospice. God had other ideas! I was hearing God's voice to do the exact thing that I didn't want to do. By then I was wide awake as I considered the prospect and a hundred questions filled my mind. However in the midst of it all I found I had peace in my heart.

Needless to say, I acted on what I'd heard and was interviewed for voluntary work. Two days later they offered me a job. Unqualified and feeling inadequate I began voluntary nursing immediately. As with everything that God calls us to do, there was grace and joy in the work. During my two years of working there I saw the Lord do some wonderful things. I was very careful not to overstep the Hospice guidelines, but was truly amazed at the number of people who initiated conversations and wanted to talk about the Lord. When we follow His lead and fulfil what He asks us to do there is always fruit for His glory.

We hear Him most often when He speaks His Word directly into our hearts. But of course there are many other ways of hearing God. He will speak to us through creation, circumstances, other people, visions and dreams etc. At times He speaks through angels or even with an audible voice, but this is rare. One of the most usual ways He chooses to speak to us is not through external things but through the impression or inner witness of His Spirit. Deep calls unto deep; God's Spirit calls to your spirit (Psalm 42:7). You know in your heart or spirit what He is communicating and may not be able to put it all into words. To develop this inner-heart hearing, we need to learn **how** to be quiet to other things and listen to His voice in our hearts.

Application

1. Silence the voice of the enemy. We see from the gospels that Jesus commanded the enemy to 'be quiet'. He has given us authority to silence the voice of the enemy too. We know from Scripture that victory over the enemy comes when we submit our lives to God. As we surrender to Him, we have authority to resist the devil and he will flee from us! (see James 4:7).

2. Silence your own soul (see Psalm 62:5 and notice that David takes command of his own soul and tells it to be quiet). He is referring to his own emotions, his mind and his will. He wants to receive from God alone and not allow himself to get in the way. A temptation in times of silence is to focus on ourselves and allow our minds to wander. If we make a decision to look at Jesus and think only about Him, then we are truly waiting on God and not on ourselves.

3. Wait in faith. Not only is David quiet but he also has an expectation – a hope – that he will receive as he waits. Imagine waiting for a train without expecting it to arrive – how ridiculous! Draw near to God and He will draw near to you. Expect God to give to you and speak to you as you wait.

> *'Have you not known? Have you not heard? The everlasting God, the Lord, the Creator of the ends of the earth, neither faints nor is weary. His understanding is unsearchable. He gives power to the weak, and to those who have no might He increases strength. Even the youths shall faint and be weary, and the young men shall utterly fall, but those who wait on the Lord shall renew their strength; they shall mount up with wings like eagles, they shall run and not be weary, they shall walk and not faint.'* (Isaiah 40:28–31)

Strength and power will come into your life as you wait in faith on God. No matter how turbulent your circumstances may be, God does not change. He is our Rock and our Refuge. To wait before Him with the revelation that your life is hidden in Christ releases His peace. He gives us everything we need to overcome in life. Emptiness and weakness are replaced by His life and strength. We are available to hear Him.

4. Listen to Him. You will hear God speak to you words of love, encouragement and faith. (Fear, condemnation and accusation are never from Him.) He may speak to you through thoughts or scriptures that come into your mind. Test everything with His Word. You can doubt that what you hear is from God and think that you are making it up, but trust that He is speaking to you. He may give you a vision or picture to show you His will and give you understanding. Be like a child and receive from your heavenly Father the good things He wants to give. Perhaps the Lord will choose not to speak but will just commune with you as you receive from His presence. Be free to receive from Him whatever He gives.

5. Write down what He speaks or shows you. It may help you to write down daily what the Lord speaks or shows you. I like to keep a record of what God has said and will take a pen and paper and write down in faith what I believe God is saying. This really helps me to listen attentively. I can test what I have heard with Scripture and see over a period of time what He has promised come to pass. (Make sure that you apply wisdom here and test what you hear with Scripture. Receive advice from more mature believers – especially if you are making decisions based upon what you are hearing.)

Note:

If you will be immersed in the Word of God and let His Word live in your heart, hearing God will be a continuous living experience and not just an occasional event. People who do not know the Word do not know the Lord well and find it more difficult to hear Him. Always acknowledge that Jesus is the living Word of God and listen to Him as you read His Word. He will speak to you very clearly and you can base your life on what He says.

Chapter 4

Practical Help for Prayer

Enemies of your prayer life

Satan attacks a believer's prayer life because prayer releases
the victory of Jesus and will produce fruit. Any person who
produces fruit for God will be opposed. So, it is wise to be
aware of the devil's tactics and identify what is happening.
Once we know the devil's schemes we can be equipped to
win.

There are also some things **we** do or don't do that can
prevent us from receiving the answers to our prayers. This
section aims to identify some of these areas and give solu-
tions from God's Word.

Unforgiveness

> *'And whenever you stand praying, if you have anything
> against anyone, forgive him, that your Father in heaven
> may also forgive you your trespasses. But if you do not
> forgive, neither will your Father in heaven forgive your
> trespasses.'*   (Mark 11:25–26)

Receiving forgiveness from God is conditional. Jesus says
that if we do not forgive others who have hurt or offended us,
we will not receive forgiveness from Him. That is a powerful
statement of truth. Unforgiveness towards others will stop
the power and blessings of God from being released into our
lives (see Matthew 18:21–35).

A certain member of my family tells a powerful testimony of the need to forgive before receiving from God. She and her family had some of their possessions stolen by a man they knew. At the same time, she was suffering with a rare nervous disorder similar to multiple sclerosis. The doctors' report was very negative and they told her that the disease was untreatable. One evening she decided to go to a Christian meeting. Before receiving from God, the preacher encouraged everyone to ask the Lord to forgive their sin and to forgive all those who had sinned against them. As she sat there, she knew she needed to forgive this man who had robbed them and to pray for him. As she prayed, the preacher had a word of knowledge about her condition and she received her healing that night.

Just as we have received God's mercy so we can be merciful to others and forgive **all** who sin against us or hurt us in any way. Bitterness and unforgiveness will 'bind' us and make us hard-hearted and unable to receive from God. Not only will it affect our prayers, but it can also have a negative effect on our mind and body.

We are to daily extend forgiveness towards those who hurt and sin against us. It is very important to realise that forgiveness is a decision and not a feeling. We choose to forgive others. Once we have forgiven, we may not necessarily **feel** any different towards them, but God will enable us to love even our enemies. As we choose to forgive and begin to pray blessing on the ones who have hurt or offended us, God's love and mercy are released through our hearts. Then we are free and receive answers.

There have been many testimonies of miracles and answers to prayer that have occurred once people have forgiven others. If you are wondering why God doesn't seem to be answering your prayers check your heart and life. Ask the Holy Spirit to show you if there is unforgiveness in your heart. Jesus said that out of the overflow of the heart the mouth speaks (Matthew 15:17–20). If you are speaking negatively or critically about someone, there may be unforgiveness in your heart. If this is the case then you need to forgive and be forgiven.

Have you noticed that at times the most difficult person to forgive is yourself? We can condemn ourselves for our own sin and failure. The Bible tells us that God does not remember our sin – there is no record of confessed sin in heaven (Psalm 103:12). We are cleansed by the blood of Jesus and can walk in His righteousness with a clear conscience (Hebrews 9:14). We are not judged or condemned. If God has forgiven us, we must forgive ourselves and choose to remember it no more.

Forgive and be forgiven. This is the sure path to successful praying.

Sin

> *'For the eyes of the Lord are on the righteous, and His ears are open to their prayers; but the face of the Lord is against those who do evil.'* (1 Peter 3:12)

Scripture tells us that those who are in Christ have become the righteousness of God. This is the gift of God and can never be earned (2 Corinthians 5:21). We are made right towards God through faith in Jesus and not by our works. However, this verse from 1 Peter tells us that God listens and responds to the prayers of the righteous, and opposes those who do evil. It matters to God that we live right. Sin hinders a believer's relationship with God and as a result, his prayer life.

> *'Beloved, if our heart does not condemn us, we have confidence toward God. And whatever we ask we receive from Him, because we keep His commandments and do those things that are pleasing in His sight.'* (1 John 3:21–22)

Confidence before God and answered prayer is assured for those who **do** the things that please God. We cannot continue to live in sin and have our prayers answered. Confidence in prayer comes when we are right with God and do the things that please Him. If we do sin, we can ask for forgiveness and depend on His mercy. But sin is not to be an acceptable part of our lives – holiness is!

Many believers confess the same sin over and over again but fail to take hold of the power to live free from that sin.

The good news is that not only can we be cleansed for our sin, we can also receive power from the Holy Spirit to enable us to live a holy life. We are not to just live as forgiven children but as victorious sons of God. We have power to overcome the desire to sin through the help of the Holy Spirit. We first **decide** not to sin and ask God to help us overcome in that particular area. Then He will help us to live free.

To win we need to get out of the way of sin. If I have a problem with anger and I watch or read things which feed this then I will most likely give in to this temptation. Even if I don't have a problem in this area and I choose to allow this to infiltrate my life through television or videos, then I could soon have a problem.

One of the most powerful examples of how to run from sin was demonstrated by Joseph (Genesis 39:10–12). Daily, Potiphar's wife attempted to seduce him. However, despite her advances he refused to give in to sin and literally ran from the room as she tried to grab him.

We need to learn to run away from temptation and refuse to give in to sin.

External discouragement

Discouragement is detrimental and can be devastating in the life of a believer. It robs joy, faith and vision resulting in apathy and failure. Thoughts like 'I don't know why I bother to pray' or 'God isn't listening anyway' fill the minds of discouraged individuals. We need to know that it is Satan that uses people to mock, accuse, hurt and undermine believers. King David experienced great opposition in his life and had every reason to be discouraged by the things people did and said about him.

> ' ... *They have spoken against me with a lying tongue. They have also surrounded me with words of hatred, and fought against me without a cause. In return for my love they are my accusers,* **but I give myself to prayer.**' (Psalm 109:2–4)

David knew that his only reliable source of help and strength came from God and so he gave himself to prayer.

We can learn a great deal from his life, particularly the way he dealt with hatred and opposition. He prayed out his problems before God and always came through to trusting God with everything. He was honest with the Lord but didn't remain in despair or self-pity.

The devil wins if we give in to self-pity, self-justification or complaining. No matter what, we must run to Jesus with our problems. There we will find grace and strength to stand in **His** righteousness alone.

It is important to remember that our battle is not against people but against the devil (Ephesians 6:12). The Word of God tells us that he is the *'accuser of the brethren'* and the *'father of lies'*. At times he may even use those closest to us to speak and act against us. We must discern the source of the attack, resist the enemy and refuse to be discouraged.

However, we must be careful, as there are occasions when the Lord will bring correction into our lives through other people. Don't be too quick to reject everything that is said, but take it to the Lord and ask Him about it. Repent if necessary and ask forgiveness if you need to.

When discouragement comes our way, our defence is faith:

> *' . . . above all, taking the shield of faith with which you will be able to quench all the fiery darts of the wicked one.'*
>
> (Ephesians 6:16)

Our faith comes from hearing God's Word. He is our shield and protection. Feed on the truth and confess it over your life. Believing and speaking the truth will extinguish the lies and accusations of the devil. As David learned to encourage himself in the Lord, we must do the same. God is your best encourager and will lift you out of discouragement and restore your heart. After all, you are who Jesus says you are and not what the enemy says!

Internal discouragement

This section deals with a problem we can all face at different times. How to expose and deal with a negative thought life.

The way we think about ourselves has a powerful influence upon us and will affect our behaviour and relationships. If we allow it, our thoughts can hinder us from living in the blessing that God has given. We can walk around with a negative image of ourselves that is based on lies from the enemy, on other people's opinions and on our own experiences in life. This wrong and damaging thinking brings discouragement and wears us out physically, spiritually and emotionally.

1. Dealing with accusation

Remember that the devil's aim is to keep us thinking negatively about ourselves. His main strategy is to accuse and remind us of our failure and sin, or to tell us that we will never be good enough. Living with a failure mentality disagrees with God's assessment of us as believers. He sees us as a success in Christ! Once we have repented of sin, we need to believe God's report about us and resist the devil and His lies. Many believers have triumphed over the accusations of the enemy by believing that God has forgiven and restored them.

> *'Therefore submit to God. Resist the devil and he will flee from you.'*   (James 4:7)

Notice that we have power and authority to resist the enemy **only** as we live in submission to God – and therefore, His Word.

> *'And they overcame him* [Satan] *by the blood of the Lamb and by the word of their testimony, and they did not love their lives to the death.'*   (Revelation 12:1)

Speaking with faith about the power of the blood of Jesus will enable you to overcome every accusation and lie. Jesus has already defeated the enemy for you. Only as you believe and speak out the victory can the accusations be overcome. Please understand that speaking aloud is an important part of your victory. Speak the Word aloud to yourself, declare it to the enemy and tell your friends! Don't be silent about all that Jesus has done for you. Your mind and attitudes will be changed as you meditate on truth and speak the Word

(Romans 12:2). Positive, Word-based thinking will protect your heart and life and you will think and act the way God wants you to.

2. Dealing with anxiety

Worry is an enemy of prayer because it brings fear and robs our faith. One anxious thought can lead to a pattern of thinking that ensnares our lives in fear and unbelief.

> *'Then He said to his disciples, "Therefore I say to you, do not worry about your life." '* (Luke 12:22)

God has made provision for us to live a worry-free life. Isn't that radical! Jesus told us not to worry because He knew we would be tempted to do so. Life has so many challenges and we often face situations that could easily produce anxiety. As soon as we start to worry or be concerned about something, we have actually begun to try and work things out ourselves and are not trusting God. Worry and fear have the potential to paralyse our faith and will succeed unless we release everything to God through prayer.

> *'Be anxious for nothing, but in everything by prayer and supplication, with thanksgiving, let your requests be made known to God; and the peace of God, which surpasses all understanding, will guard your hearts and minds through Christ Jesus.'* (Philippians 4:6–7)

This scripture is our key to freedom. In every difficult situation we are to bring our requests to God. We are not designed to carry the load and must give it in faith to Jesus. Childlike trust in our heavenly Father will bring supernatural peace into our hearts and minds.

Replace the worry with a promise

Just as our natural bodies are designed to fight disease, so the Word of God will destroy thoughts of worry and fear, bringing faith and peace. Once we have given our worries away to the Lord we must also receive God's promise of provision and victory from His Word. The Bible is full of promises and He will give us the specific one we need. Go to the Word and find a promise from your heavenly Father, who loves you and will guard, protect and provide for your life.

At times just a simple prayer is sufficient to release us from our concerns, but there are other times when we are so worried about something that we need to enter into supplication.

Supplication is a kind of prayer that pours out everything in our hearts to God until we are burden-free. It can take more time in prayer to get to a place of peace because often the issue is so deeply rooted in our hearts. The Bible tells us that one of the causes of depression is anxiety (Proverbs 12:25). We can worry about our future, health, family, finances etc. We must deal with our worries through prayer and not accept the stress and pressure that the world and devil frequently have to offer!

It really is a miracle of grace that we can be free from worry even when we face difficult and painful circumstances. I experienced this miracle whilst praying for a relative who almost died three times! The Lord healed her, but in the process I had to continually practise giving everything to Him, many times with tears, thanking Him and receiving His peace in my heart and mind.

Thanksgiving is a vital ingredient in this prayer. It gets our thinking in line with Jesus and the answer. A thankful heart will be full of faith and joy that God is good and is working His will and victory. We don't just pray to be free from worry, **we pray to get an answer** that will change the situation. The peace of God will then guard and protect our mind and heart from every attack of the enemy. We can rest in faith as we meditate on God's goodness, power and will to bring miraculous change.

3. Dealing with doubt and unbelief
These are powerful enemies of prayer because they cause us to contradict the Lord and not believe His Word. The world around us is full of thinking and opinions that oppose faith. If we accept them ourselves we will become weak, unstable Christians. It is so important that each of us regularly spend time reading, hearing and receiving God's Word. This will

remove uncertainty in our minds concerning God's will and
root out wrong thinking and ideas.

Wrong thinking about God's will produces wrong praying.
The Bible is very clear about the influence of doubt in our
lives, especially concerning prayer. Doubt actually prevents
us from receiving answers.

> *'If any of you lacks wisdom, let him ask of God, who gives to
> all liberally and without reproach, and it will be given to
> him. But let him ask in faith, with no doubting, for he who
> doubts is like a wave of the sea driven and tossed by the
> wind. For let not that man suppose that he will receive
> anything from the Lord; he is a double-minded man,
> unstable in all his ways.'*   (James 1:5–8)

This speaks about wisdom but is true for everything we
need to receive from God. Ask anything in faith, not doubting His Word or promises and it will be given. Doubt His
Word or promises and we are unable to receive. Just as the
wind tosses the waves of the sea in every direction, so doubt
makes us unstable and uncertain about what God wants to
give. Stability comes into our lives when we consistently
believe the Word above everything. The Word says that this
is **how** to receive what we ask for – in faith with no doubting!

As a child I played a game with a daisy, pulling off the
petals one-by-one, declaring with each petal 'he loves me, he
loves me not' until the last petal revealed the answer. A silly
game I know, but isn't this how we are sometimes with God
and prayer? He will, He won't, He will, He won't etc. If God's
Word says it, then we must choose to believe and not doubt.
No matter if situations don't appear to change, the Word of
God is true and He will be faithful to His Word.

Receiving from God happens as we live by faith in His
Word. Doubt can be 'put to flight' by applying the Word. Use
the Word for every circumstance, meditate and feed on it so
that your heart and mind will be filled with faith. Be single-
minded and certain about the blessings God wants to give you
through prayer, and don't waver concerning the promises.

We must be careful not to entertain or live with unbelief
and doubt in our lives. Many Christians don't realise that

unbelief is a sin. Scripture shows us that our heart is evil if it is unbelieving and does not please God (Hebrews 3:12). Repent and turn away from doubt and unbelief. Make a decision to live by faith.

Wandering thoughts

> *'But the end of all things is at hand; therefore be serious and watchful in your prayers.'*   (1 Peter 4:7)

As we pray many distractions can fill our minds – thoughts about work, friends, shopping or even food! At times it seems our mind is everywhere else but on the Lord and prayer. So, how do we combat this?

Taking command

Jesus has conquered the devil and we can now win this battle. We have been given all authority over the devil and we **can** take command of our own minds. To win we must fix our mind on Jesus – turning all our attention onto Him. Resist the enemy and he will flee. Declare that your mind belongs to Jesus.

Practically, it really does help concentration if you pray aloud. Listen to your own words and minister faith to your heart by speaking out aloud the Scriptures. A few minutes of directed, specific prayer is better than hours of wandering, unfocused prayer. If unclean or distracting thoughts do come into your mind, refuse to entertain them. Use your God-given weapons, the Word, and the blood to win.

Drowsiness and sleep

> *'But Peter and those with him were heavy with sleep; and when they were fully awake, they saw His glory and the two men who stood with Him.'*   (Luke 9:3)

We really do miss seeing the Lord and meeting with Him if we are lethargic or 'heavy with sleep'. Peter had to wake up before he could see the Lord transfigured before him. Our flesh is weak to pray and will tire easily, but the Spirit within us is willing.

> *'Watch and pray, lest you enter into temptation. The spirit is indeed willing, but the flesh is weak.'* (Matthew 26:41)

We will never make our flesh strong to pray, so there's no point in fighting it. The key to victory is to not give in to the flesh and its selfish desires but to surrender to the Holy Spirit. As we yield to the Holy Spirit, He will strengthen us to pray. We each have a choice, to yield to the flesh and 'sleep', or to the Holy Spirit and pray.

Some Christians find that whenever they go to pray they get sleepy. This can be an attack of the devil or just a matter of the flesh dominating a believer's life. The answer is to submit to God and resist the devil. Be filled with the Holy Spirit and walk, praise, shout – overcome the flesh and the devil in the power of the Spirit of God. Let the Holy Spirit be Lord of your prayer life.

All talk and no prayer

People who spend their time talking to others when they should be praying will not become strong prayer warriors. Being a friend of Jesus means that we choose Him above other friends. We must sacrifice our time and go to prayer. There is rarely a convenient time to pray and always someone you could go and talk to. Stealing God's time will reduce our effectiveness for Him and our fruitfulness.

The enemy can send people to distract us from prayer and get us into worthless conversations. Nehemiah was rebuilding the walls of Jerusalem and his enemies wanted to talk to him. His reply is wonderful:

> *'So I sent messengers to them, saying, "I am doing a great work, so that I cannot come down. Why should the work cease while I leave it and go down to you?"'*
>
> (Nehemiah 6:3)

Prayer is a great work and we must not be enticed away from it.

Wrong speaking

Once we have prayed and believe God to release His will into situations we must watch what we say. We need to agree with all we have asked and received in prayer. Talking to others can tempt us to negate our prayers and disagree with God's Word by being negative. Many people receive from God whilst they are praying but as soon as they see their friends their conversation changes and doesn't match what they left the prayer room believing. Doubt enters and hinders the answer.

Guard your tongue and speak only what you know God wants you to speak. Don't entertain other opinions in preference to God and His Word.

> *'Let the words of my mouth and the meditation of my heart be acceptable in your sight, O Lord, my strength and my Redeemer.'*   (Psalm 19:14)

Actions that assist prayer

We have just looked at some of the hindrances to prayer. But we also need to see how our prayer lives can be influenced and enhanced for good. Just as a plant can grow faster in certain conditions, so we can assist the process of growth and fruitfulness in prayer by the things we do and the environment we live in.

Body language

We see from Scripture that Jesus used His physical body during prayer. He leapt for joy, cried, and even shouted. The Bible is full of commands to shout, dance, sing, clap etc. God wants to use our bodies as we pray. (There are times for quiet prayer where we wait on the Lord and commune with Him, but even in these times our bodies can help to express what is happening.) It's the prayer of the heart that counts but body language is important. Here are some different positions and expressions that can help us in the different types of prayer:

1. Sitting

We are seated in Christ in heavenly places (Ephesians 2:6). This spiritual position reflects the rest we have in Jesus and His finished work on the Cross for us. This is the rest of faith that Hebrews 4 talks about. If you see someone sitting down it usually means they are having a rest or have finished their work. (Unless you work at a desk or with computers!) Sitting down to pray can reflect that we are relaxed and resting in God. In this position we can easily talk to and receive from the Lord.

2. Standing

Paul tells us to stand when we are dealing with the enemy (Ephesians 6:13). This symbolises that we are standing our ground and not moving from our position of victory in Christ. We don't take the enemy on sitting down, we move into action and stand up to resist him in the Name of Jesus. It really helps to physically stand whenever you are resisting the devil. It's a sign both to you and him that you mean business.

Standing can also symbolise respect towards God. If the Queen of England entered your living room you would probably feel obliged to stand and show honour and respect. There are times when it is right to stand and pray, showing the Lord that we respect His majestic presence. At other times the fervency of the prayer moves you to change physical position. Standing reveals a determination to receive God's will for a situation – and you won't take no for an answer!

3. Walking

Once again the physical action of moving your body helps to enter into different kinds of prayer. You are stirring yourself up (Isaiah 64:7) and moving, spirit, soul and body. Sometimes the lifelessness and boredom of my prayers makes me stand up, shake off the flesh and stir myself up. I walk around praising, thanking and proclaiming God's greatness. My flesh is so strong and would like to dominate me and keep me in a state of apathy! I refuse to submit to it, and move into action, believing the Holy Spirit will revive my prayers.

4. Kneeling

When we bow our hearts in humility before the awesome presence of God our bodies at times need to respond by kneeling. This physical act helps us to demonstrate more fully the submission of our hearts and lives before Him. We can do nothing but bow and acknowledge that He is Lord.

> *'Oh come, let us worship and bow down; let us kneel before the Lord our Maker. For He is our God, and we are the people of His pasture, and the sheep of His hand.'*   (Psalm 95:6–7)

5. Prostration

Lying before the Lord face down is a further act of humility and submission. It symbolises total abandonment to the God who deserves everything we are and have. This position assists a believer as they surrender everything to God. It's very healthy to know and recognise how small we are in comparison to the One we worship and serve!

6. Quiet prayer

Relationship with Jesus will mean that there are times when we just quietly talk to Him and share our hearts with Him. Entering fully into His presence brings a silent but deep communion with God and we are just loving Him and being loved by Him. Communion at this level is deeper than can be expressed with words.

7. Loud prayer

Jesus sometimes prayed loudly and so did the first disciples! Faith will often be expressed with determination and bold-ness. Being free to pray aloud all that is in your heart will release miracles. The devil wants us to be quiet and not cause a disturbance! God wants us to shout aloud and raise our voices in faith to Him. There is power released as we speak out with a loud voice. This prayer moves God to shake the natural order of things (Acts 4:31), bringing His power into the world. Strong, loud (genuine) praying indicates that we are serious about getting answers.

As we can see, our bodies are an important tool in prayer and must be used for the glory of God. These are a few examples that are found in Scripture.

The company you keep!

A believer is to live very differently from the rest of the world. Living in the right spiritual environment has a positive effect on our prayer life. Don't allow the devil to have a negative influence on you by watching wrong television programmes and videos. Be responsible and guard against the entry of the spirit of this world. If our lives are filled with the things of God we will promote the Spirit of prayer.

Make sure you are wise with the company you keep! Being with the wrong people can influence you into thinking and doing the wrong things. The Holy Spirit is grieved when we sin and make the wrong choices. Spend time with those who will love you and encourage your faith.

> *'Do not be deceived: "Evil company corrupts good habits."'*
> (1 Corinthians 15:33)

This of course does not mean that we don't spend time with the unsaved. It is the will of God to bring others to Christ through our witness. But do invest time and develop relationships with those believers who will spur you on in God. Praying with someone who has already developed a life of prayer helps us to grow faster.

Chapter 5

Effective Prayer

What is effective prayer?

> 'The effective, fervent prayer of a righteous man avails
> much.'   (James 5:16b)

The Bible shows us time and time again that incredible
power is made available by praying the right thing in the
right way. Enough power to transform entire nations! If you
and I are going to see this tremendous power working here
on earth then we need to understand how to release it.

The above scripture from James refers to a time in the
history of Israel when the Lord allowed a drought for over
three years because of idolatry in the nation. God worked
through a man called Elijah to first stop the rain, and then,
after a long season of drought, to pray for and release rain.

> 'Elijah was a man with a nature like ours, and he prayed
> earnestly that it would not rain; and it did not rain on the
> land for three years and six months. And he prayed again,
> and the heaven gave rain, and the earth produced its fruit.'
>   (James 5:17–18)

God wants us to be challenged and changed by this
scripture, seeing that one man's prayer brought about
national changes. Elijah was an ordinary man with exactly
the same human make-up as you or I. He became extraordinary by praying and receiving what God gave him. There

are immense possibilities for each of us if we pray what God
shows us to pray. We may find it easier to accept that
God will use others who are far more experienced and 'better
at prayer' than ourselves. However, the Word says that this
prayer which changes the destiny of nations is for every
believer. God wants to eliminate any small thinking or
limitations we may have regarding the impact of our prayers.
If Elijah could do it – so can we!!

One man's prayer released the will and power of God into the nation

Looking back to 1 Kings 17 and 18, we see that the Lord first
spoke to Elijah so that he would know **what** to pray. Once he
knew God's will for the nation he could pray effectively and
see the results. Today, the same principle applies. As soon as
we 'connect' with God's will and know what to ask for, it will
be done.

So, we see that the key to this earth-changing prayer is
hearing God speak. Elijah walked with God and spent time
with Him. Through knowing the Lord, Elijah understood His
purposes and **timing**. God's plan for every one of us is that
we know **what** He wants to do and **when** He wants to do it.
Spending time listening to God develops our 'spiritual ear'
and we are able to distinguish His voice above all others.

Effective prayer is hearing God and praying what you hear with faith

I remember hearing this wonderful testimony. Some parents
I know were having a few problems with their five-year-old
daughter, both at home and in school. She was becoming
argumentative, rebellious and beginning to cause lots of
trouble. Mum and Dad were praying but didn't seem to be
getting any obvious results. One morning, they listened to
the Lord and heard Him say that what their daughter needed
was a teachable heart. So they prayed and asked the Lord to
give her this heart. They got what they asked for! From that
time on their daughter has been so different. (Even the

teachers at school noticed the positive change in her – praise God!)

All effective prayer comes from hearing Him first. This doesn't mean that we will always see the immediate effect of our prayer but it does mean that it will happen in due time. We often don't know what to pray but He knows precisely what needs to happen in every situation in life. The exciting thing is that He actually wants us to know too, so that we can be co-workers with Him.

Now, both the work of the Holy Spirit and the Word are vital in our lives if we are to know God's will and not be led astray into ineffective prayer. Let's go on to look at how God speaks to us thorough His Word and through His Spirit.

Praying with the Word of God

God's will concerning everything can be discovered in His Word. The Lord has given us His will for every issue in life we could ever face, from relationships to finances, business life to bringing up children. It's in the Maker's Word! He will never act to contradict or change His written Word. Knowing and believing the Word brings confidence and security into our lives. Any person whose mind and heart are full of God's Word will be skilled and accurate in prayer. The more our prayers are filled with His Word, and therefore His will, the more fruit will be produced in prayer.

> *'Now this is the confidence that we have in Him, that if we ask anything according to His will, He hears us. And if we know that He hears us, whatever we ask, we know that we have the petitions that we have asked of Him.'*

(1 John 5:14–15)

Ask anything according to His will and you will have it!

We have His Word so that we can know Him and know what He wants to do. Without it, we would only guess about God and never really know what or how to pray. Just imagine if you didn't know that God loved you and you went by your feelings or by what other people say or do to you. Your life would be based on experience or man's opinions. The Word tells us that God has already shown His incredible love for us by giving Jesus to die in our place. Based on Scripture, we know He loves us.

Whenever we read or listen to the Word we receive life, faith, and understanding of God's will.

> *'It is the Spirit who gives life; the flesh profits nothing. The words I speak to you are spirit, and they are life.'*
>
> (John 6:63)

The living Word

God has a plan for every person and every situation. He knows the beginning and the end of all things. Even as believers we can continue to live aimless lives, wondering what life will bring. However, we live with God's plan by choosing to allow His Word to shape our thinking and destiny. His Word acts on our lives like a chisel in the hand of an expert sculptor. As we yield and let Him work, removing thinking and attitudes that aren't right, He forms our lives into His image and makes us what we have been created to be. Personally, I'd much rather be shaped and moulded by God than by this world. His work is perfect and all His ways are just! There have been times when I have resisted what He has spoken to me through His Word, usually because it's almost too good or too great to be true. But I've learned to trust that He really does know what's best for my life and future, even if it contradicts what I plan or think.

Living in daily relationship with the Word is vital for every believer, bringing us into contact and communion with Jesus. Mostly, the other things we read are just for information and we can make the mistake of reading the Word in a similar way, just to inform our minds. His Word is different – alive and full of power. If we approach God's Word with faith that He will speak and minister to us we will receive life and understanding for our lives. As a result our prayers will be more accurate and full of confident faith.

'For the Word of God is living and powerful, and sharper than any two-edged sword, piercing even to the division of soul and spirit, and of joints and marrow, and is a discerner of the thoughts and intents of the heart.'   (Hebrews 4:12)

Much of what we think has to die so that God's will can become paramount in our lives. His Word is likened to a powerful and extremely accurate sword that divides and separates what we want or think bringing revelation of God's will. Only His anointed Word can do this delicate and effective work – man can't! Essentially, His Word works in us to bring us into harmony with Him, both in prayer and in action. You and I may have some wonderful ideas about what to pray but the Lord has His plans – which are always successful and much better than ours. Whenever we receive the revelation of His will then we are ready to pray. He separates our own will from His will. Then we can **see** and **know** clearly any difference between His will and ours.

Soulish or fleshly prayers are normally filled with our experiences, opinions or ideas and are ineffective. But prayers that are born out of knowing and agreeing with the Word will produce results. We need to recognise the difference and allow the truth to sort us out.

Let's look at one practical example of how the Word changes the way we pray. In 1 Timothy 2:1–4, Paul exhorts us to pray for all men, kings and all in authority so that our cities and nations will be God-fearing and open to receive the gospel. It is clear from verse 4 that God desires **all** men to be saved and to come to the knowledge of the truth. Now, before I have the revelation of God's will, I may pray for one or two people to be saved in my family or town. (My prayer is being influenced or led by what I have experienced in the past.) However, as I meditate on the truth of God's Word I see that God desires **all** to be saved. I pray very differently now because I **know** the will of God. Jesus teaches us to pray in this way – *'Thy kingdom come, Thy will be done on earth as it is in heaven'*. To pray effectively then, I must throw out any opinions or experiences that don't agree with the Word. God wants me to ask for **all** to be saved – isn't that radical!

Praying with ideas, opinions or human limitations is not praying the will of God. We must pray what God wants. Can you see how the Word sorts out our minds and hearts to agree with Him?

Praying God's thoughts

His Word is so powerful. Everything in the universe, whether visible or invisible, has been formed and created by the Word of God. He speaks, and everything He says comes to pass.

> ' "For My thoughts are not your thoughts, nor are your ways My ways," says the Lord. "For as the heavens are higher than the earth, so are My ways higher than your ways, and My thoughts than your thoughts. For as the rain comes down, and the snow from heaven, and do not return there, but water the earth, and make it bring forth and bud, that it may give seed to the sower and bread to the eater, so shall My Word be that goes forth from My mouth; it shall not return to Me void, but it shall accomplish what I please, and it shall prosper in the thing for which I sent it." '
>
> (Isaiah 55:9–11)

God has thoughts! This means that although we can know the will of God from Scripture, which never changes, we also need to know what He is thinking and communicating today. Let me explain. I remember once sitting in a school exam busily writing an essay, quite pleased with myself, as I had revised well for that particular question. It turned out to be a good essay and would have got high marks, only I misread the question. The information I gave was right but it was the wrong answer! God's Word is always right and true, but we must tune in to God's thoughts and plans to pray the right thing. We can be like I was in that exam, forging ahead enthusiastically with a word of truth but use it at the wrong time and miss the will of God. Alternatively, we can listen and pray His thoughts which will be precisely what is needed.

Elijah was given God's thoughts and will for the nation – that the time for the rain had come (1 Kings 18:1). A year earlier would have been the wrong time as the nation wasn't ready. Now was God's appointed time for rain and Elijah knew it, believed it, and asked for it to happen. Like Elijah, we can be sensitive to hearing God's voice.

Praying for physical healing is a good example to illustrate this. Scripture is clear that it is God's will to heal (Matthew 8:3). Jesus healed **all** who came to Him. Although we may know this and so pray for physical healing, God may want to communicate something else first. Maybe the person needs a word about forgiveness, or a word that will minister faith where there is no faith. This will ultimately result in bringing about the complete healing that God wants. Remember the paralysed man who was lowered through the roof before Jesus (Luke 5:18). The first word the Lord spoke to him was about forgiveness, and then the Lord healed his body.

He knows everything and we must continuously acknowledge that His thoughts and ways are much higher that ours. We can so easily make assumptions as we pray – I have done it many times! But we must listen and tune in to God's thoughts. (See section on being led by the Spirit in prayer.)

Having two minds

The Bible tells us in 1 Corinthians 2:16 that we have the mind of Christ. It is possible for you and I to live with God's mind for every situation. But we also have our own natural mind too. Ways of thinking that can contradict the truth, as I'm sure you have noticed!

> 'And do not be conformed to this world, but be transformed by the renewing of your mind, that you may prove what is that good and acceptable and perfect will of God.'
>
> (Romans 12:2)

Wrong thinking produces wrong praying. We must learn to submit and train our minds and hearts to conform to the mind of Christ. This is a process of change that brings knowledge of His will. You and I are rather like a computer that can store information. If we store God's Word in our hearts by meditating on it day and night, we will have a deposit of truth. The more we store or save in our hearts and minds, the more there will be to draw upon. Then as we pray, the Holy Spirit 'presses the right key' and brings to our remembrance the exact scripture for that situation. Our minds become full of spiritual understanding just like a computer screen displays information.

Jesus said that this would be one of the ways the Spirit would help us (see John 14:26). He reminds us of all Jesus has said to us, the things we have heard and received into our hearts, so that we can be led into His will. Many times this has happened to me. I will be praying and a scripture will come to mind. Then as I use the Word He gives me to shape or form my prayer, I can be confident of success. Another thing Jesus said was that out of the overflow of the heart the mouth speaks. In other words, whatever is in our hearts will come out as we speak (Matthew 12:34). If His Word is stored up within our hearts, then that is what will flow out as we pray, bringing about a glorious result for the Kingdom.

Faith-filled prayers

Many people pray, but the Bible tells us that praying **with faith** gets results. It is an essential ingredient of successful prayer. Hearing God's Word personally will produce the faith we need in our hearts to believe for great things. The Lord wants to plant His Word deep into our hearts so that we have faith to believe Him and are therefore able to receive all that He desires to give.

> *'So then faith comes from hearing, and hearing by the Word of God.'*   (Romans 10:17)

> *'But without faith it is impossible to please Him, for he who comes to God must believe that He is, and that He is a rewarder of those who diligently seek Him.'*   (Hebrews 11:6)

Faith is a **gift** that comes from God. It does not come from natural things and can't be worked up or worked out – it's supernatural. Each one of us has received this gift of faith so that we can be saved (see Ephesians 2:8). We also each have a **measure** of faith that is supplied by God (Romans 12:3). This measure of faith is given to us so that we can fulfil His purposes for our lives.

2 Corinthians 4:13 also tells us that we have the **spirit** of faith by which we believe and speak. The Holy Spirit dwelling within our spirit constantly believes that all things are possible and so helps us to believe and speak faith-filled words. There is an important biblical relationship between believing in our hearts and speaking out what we believe. Our faith must be spoken through our own mouths before we can see the results of what we believe (Romans 10:9–10).

We clearly see that it is unbiblical to say that we don't have faith or can't believe. That is a lie from the enemy, designed to rob us from blessing. Many times we do need to receive faith for some specific need or purpose and can ask God to speak His Word into our hearts. By hearing the Word our faith will increase and go from strength to strength.

We have choices to make every day – either to believe God or to doubt. But as soon as we make the right choice to line up our mind, heart and will with the Word, we will be empowered to believe.

Faith is placed by God into the inner man or spirit of a believer and not into his soul (mind, will and emotions). It is solely a work of the Spirit and the implanted Word within our spirit. We receive an inner heart conviction and know that God has given us something. It's good to note here that we often **know** the things of God before we fully understand or see them actually happen.

The Word tells us that our faith is the victory. The things God has put within us that we are believing and speaking will overcome and win in the world.

> *'For whatever is born of God overcomes the world. And this is the victory that has overcome the world – our faith.'*
>
> (1 John 5:4)

Faith releases the victory of Jesus into the world and overcomes all obstacles to the will of God. Of course, our faith is not in ourselves but in God. We must never underestimate the power or value of faith and live with determination to increase in faith.

Many Christians have struggled with their ability to believe, failing to recognise that God has given them everything they need to live by faith. If you and I had faith for salvation, then we must believe that God will continue to give us faith to live the overcoming life – the life of Jesus here on this earth. After all – He does live in us!

The revivalist John Wesley emphasised the importance of faith in prayer when he said 'God does nothing on earth except in answer to **believing** prayer'. It's great to see that God has given each one of us faith, but we need to see how to put our faith into operation and get results.

How do we get our faith to work?

> *'Now faith is the substance of things hoped for, the evidence of things not seen.'*   (Hebrews 11:1)

Faith works whenever we have an assurance within our hearts that we have received something from God. We believe even before we see it with our natural eyes, and we act as though it had already happened. Think about a pregnant woman. She knows that the child is within her, even before there is any obvious physical evidence. Her life begins to change as she prepares to 'make room' for the arrival of the new baby. So true faith begins to prepare and make room for whatever you have received in your heart from God.

Noah was a hero of faith. He demonstrated that he believed God's Word by building the ark. He lived and acted as if the flood was on the way. Faith acts! Whenever we pray, God wants us to receive the answer and begin to live as though it's done. We don't live by what we see with our natural eyes, but we live by what He shows us by His Spirit and from His Word. This pleases God because it exalts His Word above everything we see in this world.

Let me share a testimony about how faith has worked in my life. During a time of prayer, the Lord spoke to me about having a new car. This wasn't my idea and so I had genuine faith from hearing His voice and not my own! I asked according to His will and thanked Him for this new car for quite a few months before I saw any evidence. I acted as though I had already received it. Because I was not on a salary but lived on gifts from travelling ministry I had to have a financial miracle. After six months the miracle happened and I was given money for a car – more than I could ask or imagine. Thank you Jesus!

Always receive what you have asked for in prayer.

> *'Therefore I say to you, whatever things you ask when you pray, believe that you receive them, and you will have them.'*
> (Mark 11:24)

Our faith needs to be activated every day and not just on special occasions. Hearing God **today** means we have faith active in our hearts to receive what God wants to give **today**. Everything Jesus has is ours. He has given us many great promises. We must act on them and make them ours.

Yesterday's faith will not do for today's prayers and needs. Don't live in past faith-failures or even successes – live by faith and pray with faith today!

Your faith will grow!

God wants to increase our faith as we walk with Him. Jesus said that nothing is impossible for us if we believe. It's faith that makes all things possible. As we continue to follow Jesus, we are to be seeing more of God's promises and Word come to pass in our lives.

Constantly **hearing** God's Word will increase your faith. Something happens to your inner man when you hear and receive the Word. A powerful change takes place and you receive the substance of things hoped for. Alive within you is the power to receive the answer or miracle that God wants to give. Only believe and you will see!

Application

1. Abide in His Word

> *'If you abide in Me and My Words abide in you, you will ask what you desire, and it shall be done for you.'* (John 15:7)

To abide means to 'live in'. Jesus wants us to live in Him and His Words to live in us. This needs to be a lifestyle and not just an occasional visit. His Word is to be alive in us everyday. How?

▷ Live each day with Jesus and begin with a fresh submission to Him and His will.

▷ Meditate and feed on His Word.

Let Him minister faith to your heart and hear what He is saying to you through His Word. To meditate means to mutter, to ponder or repeat over and over. Joshua was told by the Lord to meditate on His law day and night. Take a scripture and meditate on it; for example:

> *'Peace I leave with you, My peace I give to you; not as the world gives do I give you. Let not your heart be troubled, neither let it be afraid.'*   (John 14:27)

Speak this scripture out aloud over and over again as if the Lord is talking personally to you. Add you own name – 'Judith, My peace I give you' – remembering His Word is powerful and will accomplish what it has been sent for – you will receive faith that you have His peace.

Take other promises and words that you know God wants to **live** in your heart and meditate on them.

▷ With His Word in your heart, ask whatever you desire and it will be given to you. The Lord can trust our prayers when filled with His will.

▷ Don't allow any other words to compete with the Living Word in your heart. Then you will bear much fruit.

2. Pray His Word

This has to be one of the most effective, easiest and most powerful ways of praying. Most of us doubt our ability to pray the right way and to say the right thing, but we can't go wrong if we pray the Word of God. Every promise is yes and amen in Christ! (2 Corinthians 1:20).

▷ Prepare your heart before the Lord, and give to Him in worship and thanksgiving.

▶ Ask the Holy Spirit to lead you to a promise or scripture that is relevant for your situation. Be confident that He will guide you and show you what to pray.

▶ Meditate on the word He gives and allow the Lord to bring revelation of His will to you through that scripture.

▶ Begin to pray the scripture out loud, confess it, proclaim it, and make it personal for you and the people you are praying for.

Faith will rise as you hear yourself speaking the word. Agree with the will of God and ask for it to be done on earth as it is in heaven. God will always honour His Word.

▶ Thank God for His Word working powerfully in your life and prayers.

Some examples:

Pray **Psalm 23** over your life and family. For example:

'Lord, I thank You that you are my Shepherd, You are the One who is leading me and guiding me, my future is in Your hands. I shall not want. Lord, thank You that You are so good, so generous and kind, and that I will never want for anything because You are my God. Thank You that you lead my family, look after them and give them everything they need too. You make me lie down and rest – You have green pastures for me, places in You where I can feast in Your presence, resting in Your love and peace. Thank You Jesus that you give me rest for my soul . . . ' etc.

Pray **Colossians 1:9–14** over your life, the church you belong to, and you town or city and nation. For example:

'Lord, I pray that You will fill me with the knowledge of Your will, in all spiritual wisdom and understanding. I want to know every day the things You have prepared for me to walk in, so give me revelation of Your will for today and every day. May I understand the things You have for me to do. Lord, I pray that every brother and sister in our church will all be filled with this understanding and wisdom of Your will. May we be a people who walk in Your will daily.

Father, I pray for my city and nation, that You will pour out Your Holy Spirit and bring the people of the world to know and understand Your will for their lives. Reveal Yourself to them, show them they have a destiny and a future in you ... etc.'

Remember, this must be personal for you, from your heart. 'Weave' around the Word, bringing in other promises which the Holy Spirit will remind you of as you pray.

This is powerful prayer that receives answers **and** changes you as you pray. I personally love to pray in this way. I know it pleases the Lord and I receive such an increase in faith as I pray His Word.

3. Proclaim His Word

This is different from praying the Word in that it is a declaration and not a request. Proclaiming God's Word with faith over our lives, families and nations is a powerful thing to do. The Bible tells us to take *'the sword of the Spirit, which is the word of God'* (Ephesians 6:17) and use it to bring in God's victory.

In the beginning God **spoke** and created the heavens and the earth. He now speaks His Word through people to accomplish His purposes. This does not always have to happen in the hearing of others, but can be done alone in the prayer closet.

Proclaiming God's Word accomplishes God's will in the spirit-realm, bringing changes into the natural. Just as Jesus spoke to the storm 'be still' and we too can speak God's Word into situations of strife, violence, lack, disease etc.

'Then the Lord put forth His hand and touched my mouth, and the Lord said to me: Behold, I have put My words in your mouth. See I have this day set you over the nations and over the kingdoms, to root out and to pull down, to destroy and to throw down, to build and to plant.' (Jeremiah 1:9–10)

Jeremiah was set over the nations and given a position of authority to **speak** God's Word. The Lord told him that the result would be a tearing down of the works of darkness and a building of the Kingdom of God. His Word spoken through us has power to remove the darkness and bring in the Kingdom of Light. We live in a spiritual kingdom and are called to root out, build and plant in the spirit.

Speaking out His Word in faith will bring victory over powers of darkness. In Christ we are above all and are to bring His rule and dominion by proclaiming the Word over all things.

► Ask the Lord to give you the right word or 'sword' for the situation.

► Take it in faith and speak it aloud. Proclaim it, believe it and by faith see it accomplishing what it has been sent to do.

► Continue to use the 'sword' for as long as is necessary. Sometimes the result will be immediate and other times it will be progressive. Believe the word above everything else. Refuse to doubt. For example:

Proclaim **Ezekiel 37:3–14** to speak life and prophesy the Word of the Lord into a spiritually 'dead' situation (v. 14):

'I speak to the people in my office or workplace – in Jesus' Name – the Lord will cause you to come to life, He will put His Spirit within you and you shall live. I speak to the wind – the Holy Spirit, come and breathe on these people and they will live . . . ' etc.

Proclaim **Psalm 91** over your life and your family. I remember during one of our church prayer meetings, we were praying and proclaiming this Psalm 91 over a missionary friend who had an orphanage in Burundi. She and her children (most of them orphans from the war) were in great danger. Unless they left, terrorists were going to use violence to evict them. They had guns and grenades and intended to use them. We prayed and proclaimed this Word from Psalm 91, declaring that **no harm** would come near them. God worked and brought amazing protection and deliverance. As a result, an army of soldiers was sent to stand guard around her house. God will remove powers of darkness and even governments in answer to His peoples' prayers and proclamation of His Word.

Never underestimate the power of praying and proclaiming the Word!

Praying with the Holy Spirit

> *'But the Helper, the Holy Spirit, whom the Father will send in My Name, He will teach you all things, and bring to remembrance all things that I said to you.'*   (John 14:26)

The Father has given the Holy Spirit to all who believe in Jesus. The Holy Spirit **is** God and is equal to the Father and the Son. We can each know the Holy Spirit as a Person and not just as a vague impression or ethereal idea. He is the Spirit of Christ bringing the reality of Jesus into our lives. He is our Comforter and Helper (John 15:26) who has come to live in us and enable us to live for Jesus.

Once someone has received Christ and is born again they can ask to receive the fullness or 'baptism' of the Holy Spirit. This is God's will for everyone so that we can be equipped and empowered for service (Acts 1:5). Praying with the fullness of the Spirit of God in our lives is God's way and God's best for us. He anoints us to pray and brings life and power into our prayers. Without Him filling us, our prayers will become dull and lifeless, lacking in faith and vision.

At Pentecost the disciples were **all** baptised with the Holy Spirit, and as an outward sign they began to speak in other tongues.

> *'And they were all filled with the Holy Spirit and began to speak with other tongues, as the Spirit gave them utterance.'*
> (Acts 2:4)

Receiving the fullness of the Spirit releases the supernatural gifts of God into our lives. We must have the Holy Spirit together with every gift He brings in order to move powerfully in service for Him.

How to receive the baptism of the Holy Spirit

1.   First of all, a person must **want** to be baptised in the Holy Spirit. I know this sounds obvious, but this actually means to be immersed and filled with another Person and not with ourselves. We aren't always too willing to give up everything and allow God to be God. (Remember

that God waits for us to want Him – He works with willing hearts.)

2. Confess any known sin and receive the cleansing power of His blood. Submit your whole life to Jesus as Lord.

3. Then simply ask God to fill you with His Spirit and **receive** by faith. He gives whatever you ask according to His will.

4. Give thanks that He has given the baptism or fullness of His Spirit to you.

> *'If you then, being evil, know how to give good gifts to your children, how much more will your heavenly Father give the Holy Spirit to those who ask Him!'* (Luke 11:13)

This is not primarily an emotional experience, although your emotions may respond with joy. God's children always receive by faith. Just as the first disciples received new Spirit-given languages, so the Lord has given you the gift of a new language. It needs to flow out of you. Open your mouth and use your voice. Begin to speak from your heart as the Spirit gives you the words. Praise Him and declare His wonders in your own language and with the new language He has given you. Expect sounds to come out of your mouth that have never been learned. Don't let your mind control or stop the language of the Holy Spirit.

I'll include my testimony here because it may help. I had asked the Lord to fill me with His Spirit but there appeared to be no tangible evidence. The first word I spoke out in faith sounded so silly to me that I thought I'd made it up myself. After months of trying to find something different and more like what I'd heard others speak, I gave up. Then one day I was on my own with the Lord and I decided to start believing that I had already received the gift. I spoke a few words in faith and continued to use these words on a regular basis in prayer. As I persevered in faith the language grew in fluency and expression. Some people have an immediate fluency and others take time to develop the gift. Don't allow any unbelief or discouragement to deter you from using this precious gift.

It is important to know that we need to be filled **daily** with the Spirit. Those who have already received baptism in the

Spirit need to ask regularly to be filled afresh with Him (Ephesians 5:18).

Only the Holy Spirit can empower us and enable us to pray. Jesus is our intercessor in heaven and the Holy Spirit is our Helper and intercessor on earth, living within us. He is the life, power and inspiration of our prayers.

The Spirit of truth

Jesus called the Holy Spirit the Spirit of truth.

> *'However, when He, the Spirit of truth, has come, He will guide you into all truth; for He will not speak on His own authority, but whatever He hears He will speak; and He will tell you the things to come. He will glorify Me, for He will take what is mine and declare it to you.'*
>
> (John 16:13–14)

Once filled with the Holy Spirit, He becomes our guide or leader in prayer. He will never contradict the Word, so we can totally depend on Him to lead us into all truth. This can happen in many different ways – through a scripture, a vision, a tongue and interpretation – in whatever way He chooses. When we are 'blind' and have no understanding in prayer, we can trust Him to lead us and show us what we need to know.

So, He hears what the Father and Son are saying and declares it to us. He will only say what He has already heard and never says anything independently of the Father and Son. Everything He says or reveals to us will be in agreement with the written Word of God.

Being led by the Spirit and praying in the Spirit will mean that our prayers are full of the truth. We can know the will of God generally through the Word, but the ministry of the Holy Spirit brings the 'now' Word of God into our lives. The Spirit 'highlights' the revealed Word of God.

Prophetic prayer

Jesus also said that the Holy Spirit would tell us the things to come. How wonderful it is that the Holy Spirit knows what is ahead and will tell us what we need to know. He will have us praying things that will prepare the way for God to move in the future. You may find yourself asking for something that isn't relevant for your life now, but later on you come to understand why you prayed that way. We are an anointed, prophetic people who hear God and pray into being God's future plans.

Someone once used this illustration to describe prophetic prayer that really helped me. For a train to reach its destination, the tracks must be laid down. Without the track, the train won't come. As we pray what He reveals to us, so we prepare the way for God to move in, just like that train, with His provision and power.

Whenever the Holy Spirit speaks we can be sure that whatever He says will be successful. He never fails. Our part is to agree with Him and ask for it to be done – waiting expectantly for the answer.

What does it mean to 'pray in the Spirit'?

Paul tells us that we are to always be praying, with all kinds of prayer 'in the Spirit'. There are many different kinds of prayer found in Scripture and each type, when used correctly, will produce the necessary result. At home, I have a tool box with spanners, screw-drivers, a hammer and lots of other things I haven't learned to use yet! What I have discovered though, is that a hammer won't help if I want to tighten a screw. It's the same in my 'tool box' of prayer, there are different types of prayer, but all of them need to be used 'in the Spirit' if they are to produce the desired result.

> '. . . *praying always with all prayer and supplication in the Spirit . . .*' (Ephesians 6:18)

So, all prayer is to take place in the Spirit. Scripture tells us that we have been raised with Christ and are now hidden in Him (Colossians 3:3). If we are in Christ, Romans 8:9 tells us that the Spirit of God dwells in us and we are not in the flesh, but *'in the Spirit'*. This is good news!

> *'But you are not in the flesh but **in the Spirit**, if indeed the Spirit of God dwells in you. Now if anyone does not have the Spirit of Christ, he is not His.'* (Romans 8:9)

To be in the Spirit is, therefore, a matter of faith for a believer – taking God at His Word. This is the first step to praying in the Spirit. Faith releases us into Christ's finished work. We can't work our way to be in this position. I am not trying to be a Christian – I am. I don't try to be in the Spirit – I am.

This really will affect the way we pray. If I think I must follow some routine, sing five songs and pray in tongues for ten minutes before I'm in the Spirit, then I am adding my own work to what Jesus has done – impossible! But, by faith, I am in the Spirit and so I can sing, pray and live in the Spirit.

This does **not** mean, as you well know, that we always live out our lives in the Spirit. We say things, do things and sometimes pray things that are definitely not in the Spirit. But, as we apply faith that we are in the Spirit, we will flow from the power of our position in Christ.

Secondly, an important part of praying in the Spirit is to have the right mind-set. Right thinking leads to right praying. We need to understand that our mind plays an important part in co-operating with the work of the Holy Spirit. Just as a door can open to allow us into another room, so the mind acts like a door that can swing us from the 'room' of the Spirit, where God has placed us, and into the 'room' of the flesh. If we allow ourselves to think worldly thoughts we will move into the flesh and our prayers will be hindered.

> *'For those who live according to the flesh set their minds on the things of the flesh, but those who live according to the Spirit, the things of the Spirit. For to be carnally minded is death, but to be spiritually minded is life and peace.'*
>
> (Romans 8:5–6)

Fill your mind with His Word as you pray and confess the truth that He has given you the mind of Christ. Don't lean on your own understanding (Proverbs 3:5–6) or open the door to fleshly prayers. Think right and you will pray right and be able to pray in the Spirit with your mind on heavenly things!

Pray from the river

> ' "He who believes in Me, as the Scripture has said, out of his heart will flow rivers of living water." But this He spoke concerning the Spirit, whom those believing in Him would receive; for the Holy Spirit was not yet given, because Jesus was not yet glorified.' (John 7:38–39)

Jesus said that the Holy Spirit would be like 'rivers of living water' flowing out of our hearts. Having faith in Jesus releases the powerful river of the Spirit.

God's Spirit flows from a believer's heart (spirit or inner man), and continues out through his soul and body. The word 'belly' is another translation for heart. Out of our bellies – deep within us – the life of God will flow. There needs to be an outlet for this river, and God has chosen to use our faith together with our voices to release His power. Otherwise the river becomes like a dam inside a believer, restricted and stationary. Our mouth is the 'tap' which when opened will release the water of life.

> **Prayers in either our natural language or in our spiritual language that start from our inner man are prayers in the Spirit.**

We can choose to operate from reasoning or intellect (the flesh) in prayer and spend our lives dominating or quenching the Holy Spirit within us, or we can pray from the river within us – **in the Spirit**.

There are some things that only our spirit knows. Things the Lord has put deep within us that our minds haven't yet understood. God communicates with and through our spirit-man. We can pray in the Spirit by using our prayer language, His Word or the other spiritual gifts He gives. The Holy Spirit knows what is needed and can effectively communicate these things through us to the Father in prayer.

Many times we don't know what to pray. The Holy Spirit will help us by giving us what needs to be prayed. He takes hold of situations together with us, releasing power to bring about His victory. This may be in the form of our own language or with languages and sounds that we don't understand with our minds – even groans, sighs and tears. Our part is to trust and believe that God is accomplishing His will through us by using our faith, voices and yielded hearts and minds. Turn the tap on and the river of life will flow.

> *'Likewise the Spirit also helps us in our weaknesses. For we do not know what we should pray for as we ought, but the Spirit Himself makes intercession for us with groanings which cannot be uttered. Now He who searches the hearts knows what the mind of the Spirit is, because He makes intercession for the saints according to the will of God.'*
> (Romans 8:26–27)

Praying in the Spirit in this way will enable you to enter into the miraculous power and provision of God. The words or expressions that are released will be exactly what is needed.

Being led by the Spirit in prayer

> *'For as many as are led by the Spirit of God, these are sons of God.'*   (Romans 8:14)

Our heavenly Father calls every believer a son of God. This means that we all have the same rich inheritance in Christ. Now, to actually live as a son we need to be led by the Holy Spirit. Being led means you are moving and going somewhere and not just standing still. When we place the Lord 'in the driving seat' of our lives, He determines what will happen and where we are going.

> *'For you did not receive the spirit of bondage again to fear, but you received the Spirit of adoption by who we cry out, "Abba, Father". The Spirit Himself bears witness with our spirit that we are children of God.'*   (Romans 8:15–16)

We have received the Spirit of adoption and it is through Him that we have revelation in our spirits and know that we are sons of God. He bears witness with our spirit the truth that we are healed, we are loved, we have power, we have joy, etc. By Him dwelling in us we cry out 'Father'. We **know** we belong to Him and He is our Father, even if we find it difficult to grasp with our minds.

Just as we know these things deep within our hearts by the work of the Holy Spirit, so we are led by Him to know what He wants us to pray. We know it from our spirit, which the Bible also calls a lamp. He illuminates our spirit so that we can see.

> *'The spirit of a man is the lamp of the Lord, searching all the inner depths of his heart.'*   (Proverbs 20:27)

The most common way to be led by the Lord is from within our spirit-man and not by external events, voices and circumstances. (Although He can speak to us externally and through circumstances.) His Spirit bears witness with our spirit the things He wants to say and do. He lights up our spirit with revelation of His will. Revelation comes before understanding! Remember this when you are praying. It may be a while before your mind understands what God is doing, but go with what you know in your spirit.

Our spirit has been created by God to dominate and lead our soul and body. He has chosen to communicate to our spirit and then our minds can be informed. We need to develop our spirit and learn to be led only by God's leading within and not our own soulish reactions and responses. Many of us, and I include myself, have lived so long in body- or soul-dominated lives that we have to re-train ourselves to respond primarily to our spirit, of course, testing everything to agree with God's Word.

> *'Now we have received, not the spirit of the world, but the Spirit who is from God, that we might know the things that have freely been given to us by God.'*   (1 Corinthians 2:12)

The Holy Spirit speaks to us in many ways using impressions, dreams and visions, scriptures etc. If He chooses to speak words to us, His voice within can sometimes sound like we are talking to ourselves. We learn to discern the difference between our own voice and His by knowing His Word, His purposes and character. Jesus promised that His sheep would hear and know His voice and follow Him (John 10:4). Every believer is designed by God to hear and know His voice.

For example, He may impress upon us the need to pray for a missionary in another country or we may see someone's face in a vision. Other times we can 'sense' a need to pray for a certain person. This is all being led by Him. Obey His voice or prompting and there will be fruit. Of course, not every thought, vision and impression that comes to us is from God. But the more we know Him and His ways, the more confident we become both in recognising and responding to Him.

Remember that we don't need to fear the enemy. God gives us discernment and the wisdom we need as we pray. Jesus is the Good Shepherd who leads us in peace and victory. The enemy is easily recognised as he brings doubt, condemnation, despair and pressure.

When you have the witness of the Spirit within, then you know that you are on the right track with God. There will be life in that prayer and joy that comes from sharing in God's work. Just as the baby leapt inside Elizabeth's womb in response to the Child in Mary (Luke 1:41), so our spirits will witness and respond to what God is doing.

One key to being led by the Holy Spirit in prayer is to lay down our own thoughts or agendas, and **believe** that He will lead. Pray out of your inner man and go with the witness of the Spirit. This is a learning process and will always require faith. Just trust Him.

Very often, this leading will not necessarily be a definite statement that you hear, for example 'Pray for Jean'. But there will be a prompting within you. Go with your inner man, with what you sense God is leading you into. More understanding will come as you begin to move in faith.

Many times I really don't know where to begin, but as I yield to Him, trust Him and start to pray, He will lead me. Remember that the Holy Spirit flows like a river and we cannot predict where He is going. We just need to allow Him to lead and go on this exciting journey with Him.

Test your prayers

There are a few ways we can test and see if our prayers are being led by the Spirit. Ask yourself a question. If Jesus were praying now, would He be asking for the same things? Listen to your words and make sure they agree with God's Word.

We know that the Spirit will never be negative, or lead to despair and hopelessness. He won't lead us to pity ourselves, to be discouraged or feel useless. He will not have us dwelling on the problem, but have us praying the answer. Even when we are going through difficult times, He will lead us in victory, joy and peace. He brings healing and will reveal all the positive things that are ours in Christ. He won't let us dwell on the past, but will show us the new thing He is doing and always lead us to believe for the impossible!

Application

1. Repent of any known sin and ask God to fill you with His Spirit.

2. Receive by faith and give thanks for all the ways He works in and through your life.

3. Believe that you are in the Spirit, and set your mind on Jesus and His will. Submit your thoughts to Him and thank Him that He has given you His mind.

4. Pray in tongues and in your own language. Let the prayer flow from the life of God within you. Jesus said that the rivers of living water would flow from within as you believe in Him. Faith releases the life of the Holy Spirit. Pray like this in the Spirit for at least ten minutes, believing God's life is flowing as you pray.

5. Ask Him to show you what to pray for. Let Him lead you and by faith, yield to His Word, impressions or visions. Pray out whatever He gives you. If He reminds you of a scripture as you are praying, use it to ask for His will in whatever situation He has led you to pray for.

6. Once you know that you have received what you have asked for, wait for Him to lead you on to pray for another situation. Of course, if you have something already on your heart, present this to Him and let the Spirit lead you into effective prayer for that situation.

   Sometimes it's good to record what you prayed and how you prayed for future reference and encouragement.

7. Praise Him that whatever He has shown you will be done, and finish your prayer with thanksgiving.

Note:

For more teaching on praying in the Spirit see the section on 'Different types of prayer'.

'Hot' prayers get results

> *'The effective, fervent prayer of a righteous man avails much.'*   (James 5:16b)

In the previous sections of the chapter we have been looking at what it means to pray effectively. Now, Elijah not only prayed effectively, but Scripture tells us his prayer was earnest and fervent.

Imagine you are in a cold house in winter with no central heating. There's plenty of wood in the fireplace, but nothing to light it with. How unfortunate! If heat is going to be produced then you must have both fuel **and** fire. There is a winning combination that gets results in prayer – effective **and** fervent. One without the other just doesn't produce the results.

Fervent actually means to be hot, full of heat, having or showing great desire and emotion. Notice that Elijah wasn't casual in his response to the Word of the Lord to send rain, as if it were a nice idea. He embraced it in his heart and prayed strong, faith-filled, 'hot' prayers. His prayers were full of passion and desire to see the will of God done on earth. Elijah was determined to get results.

In the Old Testament we see that Scripture likens prayer to sweet-smelling incense. In the Temple incense was burned by the priest on the altar close to the veil that separated the Holy Place from the Holy of Holies. This incense was symbolic of constant prayer being offered up to God (see Exodus 30:6–8). Without fire, the incense would not burn and ascend before the Lord.

It's the same with the prayers we bring before God's throne. If there is no fire, no heat or desire for the answer, then our prayers lack power.

Casual, cold and disinterested prayers will not move God to act. Scripture shows us time and time again that He responds to the genuine cries of His people. Blind Bartimaeus cried out so loud above the crowds that it stopped Jesus in His tracks. Desperation often leads to fervent praying. This blind man was not going to allow Jesus to move on without blessing him. That is fervent, determined and powerful prayer, and he got his miracle (Mark 10: 46–52).

The fire of God

We need fire and heat in our hearts when we pray. Hearts that are aflame with the will of God. This fire comes from the passion God creates within our hearts by His Word and Spirit. Whenever we are gripped by God's will and plans, it is easy to pray with earnest, heart-felt desire. The Holy Spirit gives us passion so that we can pray fervently.

If we yield to Him and are filled with His Word and Spirit, He will put fire in our hearts. Then we are 'caught up' with Him and His plans, totally united with His will. We are free to be bold and cry out aloud, like Bartimaeus, declaring that we will not let Him go until we see what He has promised.

Of course, noisy prayer is not always a sign that the prayer is fervent. We can pray fervently but quietly and we can pray loudly, but with no real heart engagement. If we don't connect with God's heart, volume in itself becomes an empty method.

However, loud prayer is scriptural and necessary. As God's passion ignites our hearts, fire will produce heat and our prayers will ascend to Him from our spirit, through our souls and out of our bodies.

> *'But His Word was in my heart like a burning fire shut up in*
> *my bones; I was weary of holding it back, and I could not.'*
>   (Jeremiah 20:9b)

Jeremiah had the Word of the Lord burning in his heart, to the point where he couldn't keep quiet. That's what God wants in our prayers: His Word to be so strong within us that it bursts out of us as we pray with passion.

Old way – new move

Fervent prayers full of passion and fire are not new. Jesus prayed like this in the garden of Gethsemane. If we look at 1 Samuel 1:1–20 in the Old Testament, we see that a woman called Hannah was desperate for a child. She knew that talking to man wouldn't change anything; she had to go to God. She got up, went to the temple and prayed with such intensity that Eli the priest thought she was drunk! The outward appearance was misinterpreted, but God knew what was reaching Him from her heart. Out of this woman's fervent prayer came Samuel, a miracle child who was raised to be God's chosen vessel for revival in Israel. Now, I am sure that Hannah had prayed many times for children, but the miracle happened when she became desperate and fervent in her prayer.

It's exciting to hear and see the changes that are taking place in the Church worldwide. Prayer meetings are no longer subdued or quiet places to go. God is birthing a holy desperation in His Church to see revival and multitudes brought out of darkness. The Church is once again praying fervently and often loudly for a harvest of souls and for God's will to be done in the earth. This is an old way (Acts 4) but new passion and vision is stirring within the hearts of God's people for His Kingdom to come. The fire is increasing and so is the power. Fervent, 'hot' prayers are ascending before the throne and God is answering with miracles. Let the Word and the Spirit create a new fire within you for the will of God, so that the cry of your heart is:

> *'Your kingdom come, your will be done on earth as it is in*
> *heaven.'*   (Matthew 6:10)

Application

Using these scriptures allow the Lord to put His Word deep into your heart. Meditate on His Word. Yield to Him and receive His passion and vision.

'Violence shall no longer be heard in your land, neither wasting nor destruction within your borders; but you shall call your walls Salvation, and your gates Praise.'

(Isaiah 60:18)

'Then the eyes of the blind shall be opened, and ears of the deaf shall be unstopped. Then the lame shall leap like a deer, and the tongue of the dumb shall sing. For waters shall burst forth in the wilderness, and streams in the desert.'

(Isaiah 35:5–6)

'And the glory which You gave Me [Jesus] *I have given them,* [believers] *that they may be one just as We are one.'*

(John 17:22)

Now pray for the nation and the Church using these scriptures with fervent desire to see His will done on earth. Your effective, fervent prayers will make tremendous power available.

Chapter 6

Different Types of Prayer

This chapter is intended to be an easy reference guide to various types of powerful and effective prayer. They can be used individually, in a group, or as a whole church.

The prayer of agreement

Definition

In this type of prayer two or more believers agree together for the will of God to be done here on earth as it is in heaven.

Foundational scripture

(Please read Matthew 18:1–20)

> *'Assuredly, I say to you, whatever you bind on earth will be bound in heaven, and whatever you loose on earth will be loosed in heaven. Again I say to you that if two of you agree on earth concerning anything that they ask, it will be done for them by My Father in heaven. For where two or three are gathered together in My Name, I am there in the midst of them.'* (Matthew 18:18–20)

Jesus placed great value on the prayer of agreement, where believers come together in His Name, at one with Him concerning His will. Living in this agreement they have power to stop everything that hinders His will. They can also loose or permit whatever is His will and agree in prayer concerning **all** things. This shows us that Jesus intends believers to influence every aspect of life on this earth by releasing His government or rule.

What you need to know before you pray

1. All prayer is to agree with God's will

> *'Now this is the confidence that we have in Him, that if we ask anything according to His will, He hears us.'*
>
> (1 John 5:14)

Here is the basis and the confidence for our prayers – anything according to His will. Before we can agree in prayer together, we must first find out and agree with God.

2. What is agreement?

Agreement with God is more than just mentally assenting to His will in prayer. True agreement affects our whole lifestyle. If God asks me to do something and I reply 'Yes, Lord', but don't do what He asks, then that is not agreement. I may **mentally** acknowledge His Word but if I am to be in true agreement with Him I will live His Word. Spiritual agreement must affect our spirit, soul and body as believers. Every part of my being is to demonstrate agreement with Him. My spirit first receives revelation of His will and then my mind, will, emotions and body submit and agree.

In Matthew 18:19 the word 'agree' actually means 'to be in harmony or symphony'. A musical orchestra will sound terrible if half are playing Mozart and half Beethoven. At times when we pray with other believers, we can be playing a completely different 'tune' to the others and definitely not be in harmony. Every available instrument (spirit, soul, and body) needs to come together in agreement with God, both individually and then corporately. Now that is agreement!

3. Agreeing together

The will of God must be known before we can agree together. There are many things we already know to be the will of God, and so we can pray immediately with faith and conviction in our hearts. For example, we know that God has provided health, peace, joy, and everything we need for life. We can believe and agree with others for His best in these areas. However, if someone asks me to pray with them about finances for a house in the Bahamas, I cannot until I personally have the witness of the Spirit for this prayer. I know this is a silly example but many people can ask you to agree with their soulish desires and not with God's will. I **can** pray with them for confirmation of God's will but I cannot agree in prayer until I know in my own heart that this is what God wants to do. When each person has faith in their heart, which comes from personally hearing and knowing God's will, then we are ready to pray together.

4. Three lifestyle foundations for agreement
Before Jesus taught specifically on the prayer of agreement He gave three important keys that release the power of agreement (see Matthew 18:1–17).

► *Humility*

In Matthew 18:1–5 the disciples ask Jesus a question: 'Who is the greatest?' This question is, sadly, still asked in the Body of Christ today – who's the best singer, preacher, pastor etc. – and will only promote competition and division. Our flesh constantly jostles for position and recognition. This is pride and will prevent the release of God's power into our lives and through our prayer together. Pride is sin and it separates us from God and from others. Jesus teaches that humility is a key for greatness as it brings us into agreement with His will and others who serve Him. We must be changed and become like children who are dependent and trusting Him. A humble people can live together in agreement with God.

True humility is simply agreeing with the Word. If He says you are anointed, more than a conqueror and a son, then you accept it. That is not pride! Humbling ourselves and making ourselves 'low' before Him opens our hearts for change. If we have an attitude 'I know I'm right and everyone else is wrong' then perhaps we need to submit ourselves to the Lord and ask for His guidance. We are of course not to compromise God's Word, but are to be willing to change if we are wrong and be conformed to His will. This heart humility will help others to seek God with you for His will. Humility brings power into the prayer of agreement.

▶ *Holiness*

Matthew 18:6–9 is a radical passage of Scripture about how we should deal with sin. No matter how painful it may be, we are to cut all sin out of our lives. Sin breaks fellowship and agreement with God and affects our prayers with other believers. We are warned not to lead others into sin, for example gossiping and criticising others. Jesus says this will lead to destruction. All sin is forgiven if we confess it before God and turn away from it (1 John 1:7–9). It has no dominion over us in Christ. When we repent, we are restored, forgiven and made holy in His sight. A holy lifestyle brings power into the prayer of agreement.

▶ *Forgiveness and reconciliation*

Continuing to teach His disciples (Matthew 18:10–17), Jesus emphasises the need for us to have His heart for those who are lost or go astray. We are not to judge them, but reach out with mercy and love. Jesus came to save and not to condemn.

In a situation where one believer sins against another, the Word shows the right way of dealing with it that promotes unity and agreement. The one who has been sinned against is not to immediately pick up the 'phone and tell their friends what happened! They must go directly to the one who has sinned and seek reconciliation so that the offence doesn't spread and damage the unity of the Body. If there is no repentance and reconciliation then he is to take one or two others, (preferably mature believers or leaders) to win his brother back to unity and agreement. Notice that the purpose is to preserve agreement through forgiveness and not prove that you were right. Can I just add here that this is intended for serious issues of division and disagreement, not for small details of offence. For example, we can all feel ignored or rejected at times, but we must choose to forgive quickly and get on living for Jesus. However, in a serious situation where the leaders are brought in to resolve the situation, if there is no repentance or change then Scripture tells us to bring it before the whole church. The aim of this is to give more opportunity for repentance. Remember always that we are not under law but grace and God desires mercy. If that believer's sin continues to affect the whole body negatively and he or she still refuses to repent, the leadership have authority to ask them to leave the church. Sin and unforgiveness will grieve the Holy Spirit and hinder the work of the Kingdom. God is jealous for unity in His Church and we must protect it. Forgiveness and reconciliation brings power into the prayer of agreement.

5. Agreement with others brings supernatural increase in power

> '*When the day of Pentecost had fully come, they were all with one accord in one place. And suddenly there came a sound from heaven, as of a mighty rushing wind, and it filled the whole house where they were sitting.*' (Acts 2:1–2)

The believers were together in one heart and one mind when God poured out His Spirit. There is a connection here with believers being united and a move of God. Great outpourings of the Spirit have continued to happen as believers have come together in one heart and mind agreement with God.

Deuteronomy 32:30 tells us that there is a supernatural increase in power for deliverance from the enemy when the people of God come together in agreement. If one can 'chase a thousand, and two put ten thousand to flight', then incredible deliverance is possible through the united Church of Jesus Christ.

6. Power to bind and loose

To bind means to stop or prevent something from being able to operate. Jesus says we have power to bind on earth anything that has already been bound by Him through His work on the Cross. We see that there is no sickness, sin or oppression in heaven. There is no deception, corruption or murder. Together we can bind all that contradicts His will here on earth. To loose means to untie or let go everything that was loosed for mankind through the Cross. The Church has authority to loose heaven here on earth – health, right-eousness and salvation etc. We agree with God and each other to see heaven invade the earth. God moves in response to our action and agreement with Him.

Notice that God waits for us to bind and loose. It's not something we pray and ask Him to do. Here are some examples:

Bind	*Loose*
False religion/deception	Spirit of revelation and truth
Fear	Love/boldness
Doubt	Faith
Addictions (drugs/alcohol)	Liberty/freedom
Infirmity/disease	Healing
Pride	Humility
Death	Life
Control/manipulation	Freedom in the Spirit

7. Faith must be operating
As we agree in prayer, we must apply faith and believe that whatever we ask in His name will be done. The Lord promises His presence as we agree in His name, representing His authority, character and will.

Application

Make sure that your heart is right before the Lord. Submit and humble yourself before Him, confess any sin and make a decision to remove all compromise. Receive His cleansing and grace to be holy as He is holy. Forgive others and pursue reconciliation in the body of Christ.

1. Humble yourself to receive God's will for a specific situation.

2. Before you start to pray make sure that everyone knows God's will and is in agreement and faith.

3. Being led by the Spirit, use your authority and speak aloud together to bind everything that opposes God's will. Then loose the will of God. For example, 'In Jesus Name we bind every spirit of rebellion and blindness and loose the Spirit of revelation and faith.'

4. Then pray and ask God to bring His will into those areas. Be specific with your requests and believe. For example:

   'Father, together we agree concerning our local school. We ask for the head teacher to be saved. We pray that the gospel will be preached to every child and that every ear will be opened to hear Your voice. We pray for labourers to be sent out into this harvest field so that souls will be reaped for the glory of Your Name. Amen!'

5. Together give praise and thanksgiving to the Lord.

Note:

As we live together in this 'lifestyle of agreement' God's rule will come with power through His Church. We are to spiritually govern and rule our cities, villages and workplaces for God through binding, loosing and agreeing together in prayer. Nothing is impossible as we believe and agree – incredible power is released!

Praying with other tongues

Definition

Praying in tongues is a spiritual prayer language given to every Spirit-filled believer (Ephesians 1:3). With this gift a believer is able to communicate and pray directly from his spirit or inner man to God. He speaks using sounds, expressions or languages that are God-given and not learned with his mind.

Foundational scriptures

'And they were all filled with the Holy Spirit and began to speak with other tongues, as the Spirit gave them utterance.'

(Acts 2:4)

> *'For if I pray in a tongue, my spirit prays, but my under-
> standing is unfruitful. What is the conclusion then? I will
> pray with the spirit, and I will also pray with the under-
> standing. I will sing with the spirit, and I will also sing with
> the understanding.'*   (1 Corinthians 14:14–15)

What you need to know before you pray

1. This is a gift for you to use

We need to use every gift that enables us to live in God's
supernatural power. Once filled with the Holy Spirit a
believer is to see this gift **released** and operating in his or
her life (see Luke 11:13 and Chapter 5 on 'How to be baptised
in the Spirit'.) This gift can be a doorway to the other gifts of
the Spirit. As the river of the Spirit begins to flow through
tongues, words of knowledge, wisdom, healing etc. can also
begin to flow.

Paul says in 1 Corinthians 14:15 *'I will pray with the spirit'*
which shows us that Paul exercised his own will to pray in
tongues. He didn't wait for occasions when he 'felt' like it or
was 'overcome' with the anointing. Once we are baptised in
the Spirit, the gift is there to be used whenever we choose.
Paul also mentions that he was glad he spoke in tongues
more than everyone else (1 Corinthians 14:18). He obviously
highly valued the gift of tongues in his prayer life.

2. A tongue speaks to God

> *'For he who speaks in a tongue does not speak to men but to
> God, for no one understands him; however, in the spirit he
> speaks mysteries.'*   (1 Corinthians 14:2)

When we speak in tongues our spirit speaks to God and He
understands what is being said. We are not addressing or
speaking to the enemy. However, this does not mean that the
enemy is unaffected by this kind of prayer. Tongues will
release the power of the Spirit and bring the will and
purposes of God as we pray. Therefore the enemy will be
defeated.

3. Praying in tongues makes you spiritually strong

'He who speaks in a tongue edifies himself.'
(1 Corinthians 14:4)

'But you, beloved, building yourselves up on your most holy faith, praying in the Holy Spirit.' (Jude 20)

Praying in tongues will build supernatural strength into your life with God. When praying in tongues, apply faith that this is happening according to the Word – you are being edified! We need God's Spirit to strengthen us in our inner man so that we can operate daily out of the power of the Spirit within us (Ephesians 3:16).

4. Tongues magnify God

'We hear them speaking in our own tongues the wonderful works of God.' (Acts 2:11)

Our own language can seem to be rather limited in praise and worship. We can use this gift to express praise and adoration in personal worship. At times we can be praising Him in languages that other people understand but we have never learned! The Holy Spirit knows when people need to hear about how wonderful Jesus is in their own language.

I was once leading a public prayer meeting and was speaking in tongues and English, releasing my praise and heart to the Lord. A lady walked in the back of the building and heard me speaking tongues in her dialect of Zambian, 'Lord, You are wonderful, and I welcome You in this place'. Of course I had no idea until she told me after the meeting. I had been declaring the wonderful works of God in other languages.

During corporate times or alone with God we can use this gift to worship and praise Him.

5. The Holy Spirit is our Helper

'Likewise the Spirit also helps us in our weaknesses. For we do not know what we should pray for as we ought, but the Spirit Himself makes intercession for us with groanings

which cannot be uttered. Now He who searches the hearts knows what the mind of the Spirit is, because He makes intercession for the saints according to the will of God.'

(Romans 8:26–27)

We are weak in prayer but the Spirit helps us to pray with sounds, expressions and languages we don't understand. We often don't know what to pray or even how to pray, but if we allow the Spirit to pray through us, our weakness is replaced with His strength. The Bible tells us that when the Holy Spirit prays through a believer it is according to the will of God. We can be sure we are praying accurately.

As we yield to Him, we become a vehicle through which His will is accomplished in prayer. Sounds or groans expressed through us are bringing His will and purposes to pass. The key to success is that no matter what language or expression is being released through our hearts and mouths, we **believe** that He is accomplishing His will. Pray with faith. (See 'The prayer of intercession' in this chapter for further study.)

7. Hearing God through interpretation

'Therefore let him who speaks in a tongue pray that he may interpret.'   (1 Corinthians 14:13)

Whilst praying in tongues we need to be sensitive to what is happening in our spirit. The more the gift of tongues is used the more open and sensitive we become to spiritual things. As we pray we can ask the Lord to reveal to us and interpret what we are praying. Understanding will help us to join with His work and also encourages our faith.

Interpretation is not the same as translation. We **know** or **sense** in our spirit what is happening as we pray often without understanding all the details. Our mind can also receive information from the Holy Spirit as He gives understanding. This helps us pray in our own language too and maintains vision and purpose. Develop your ability to move with the witness of the Spirit and receive the interpretation of your prayer language by practising. You may know that certain things are happening whilst you are praying or you may need to stop and listen to God. Interpretation doesn't happen all the time. We need to pray in faith at times when we have no idea what specific things are taking place. However, do expect to receive interpretation as you ask.

Application

1. Ask and receive the fullness of the Spirit by faith. If you haven't spoken in tongues before, thank God for giving you this gift through His Spirit within you. Simply believe.

2. Exalt and praise Him using your own language and the spiritual language He gives you. Believe Jesus and keep your focus on Him. Speak whatever He gives you to speak.

3. Now, strengthen your inner man and pray aloud in tongues with faith. Believe that God is building strength into your inner man. Let the prayer come from deep within you – loud, strong and bold. Do this daily beginning with ten minutes. Of course, the more you pray, the stronger you will be – so increase the time spent praying in tongues at will.

4. Ask for the interpretation. You may want to pray for a situation, but don't know what to pray. Use the gift of tongues and begin to pray, asking for interpretation. You may sense a need to pray specifically with your own language. Pray whatever He gives you and listen to Him. He will lead you in faith and victory as you pray.

   When you don't have a specific request but just want to be led by God, begin by yielding to Him and start to pray in tongues. Continue until you 'catch' something in the Spirit and then pray as He leads. Be free to move into different expressions and don't be limited by just one sound or language. The Holy Spirit will give you a variety of sounds and languages to accomplish His will.

Praying with the understanding

Definition

To pray with understanding means to pray with revelation knowledge of the will of God. In this prayer our minds are brought into agreement with God's mind and purposes. This type of prayer is not just with the mind, but flows out from the life of the Word and leading of the Holy Spirit within a believer.

Foundational scripture

> 'For if I pray in a tongue, my spirit prays but my under-standing is unfruitful. What is the conclusion then? I will pray with the spirit, and I will also pray with the under-standing. I will sing with the spirit, and I will also sing with the understanding.'   (1 Corinthians 14:14–15)

What do you need to know before you pray?

1. Your mind is important in prayer
Paul teaches that praying solely with the gift of tongues can leave our minds to wander and be unfruitful. So, he makes a decision to pray using both types of prayer. *'I will also pray with the understanding...'*

It can take more effort to pray with our understanding than with tongues. We can speak in tongues for hours and not use our minds. Whilst this prayer is going on, we can dream about holidays in the sun or the menu tonight! The best and most fruitful way is to use both understanding and tongues. This helps us to be totally involved with the prayer. If our thoughts are wandering we will soon lose interest and give up. Pray using your mind and not just your spirit and train yourself to be skilled in this type of prayer.

2. Praying the Word
Always take the Bible with you when you pray and use the Scriptures in prayer. If your mind wanders then read aloud and pray the Word.

3. 'Lost in the Spirit'

At times we can be so taken up with Him in the Spirit as we pray. Being 'lost' in the Spirit means that we become more conscious of God and spiritual things than natural things. Here we will pray out things with our understanding that our minds haven't ever thought about. The Lord gives revelation and inspiration that we have never heard before. We will be prophesying and praying His will in prayer (John 16:13).

It is easy to pray in the Spirit using both tongues and understanding for long periods of time if you surrender the time and agenda to Him. This prayer is so exciting you will not want to stop!

Application

1. Submit to Jesus and ask to be filled with His Spirit. Receive by faith and praise and thank Him.

2. Be led by the Spirit and take a scripture to pray out over your life or circumstances. Don't look for a thunderbolt from heaven to guide you – go with the witness you have. Involve your heart as you talk to God and speak to Him from that word. Move from tongues into under-standing and be free to pray out what God shows you.

   If you are a new Christian and starting out in prayer it will help to keep the Scriptures open and in front of you so that you can see the Word you are praying. The more you know the Word the easier praying with the under-standing will be. Eventually you will be able to pray from the 'storehouse' of the Word in your heart. The Holy Spirit will remind you of what Jesus has said as you yield to Him (John 14:26).

3. Focus your mind and heart on Jesus and give up your own agendas. Be God-conscious and let Him lead you. Really enter into the prayer by faith and give Him every-thing. Be completely abandoned to His agenda.

   As He leads you, just follow Him and pray out whatever understanding you have. Once you have finished you may want to write down some of the things you heard yourself praying and keep a journal. Whatever is from God will come to pass. Test everything with the Word and believe that God's will has been done on earth as it is in heaven!

The prayer and command of faith

Definition

In commanding prayer (sometimes called the prayer of faith) we not only pray to God but also speak directly to change situations and remove demonic powers and obstructions. In this type of prayer, a believer must first agree with the revealed will of God and then take direct authority to remove anything that obstructs His will on earth. Once all hindrances are out of the way, he asks and receives what God wants to give by faith.

Foundational scriptures

'Now the next day, when they had come out of Bethany, He was hungry. And seeing from afar a fig tree having leaves, He went to see if perhaps He would find something on it. When He came to it, He found nothing but leaves, for it was not the season for figs. In response Jesus said to it, "Let no-one eat fruit from you ever again." And His disciples heard it.'

(Mark 11:12–14)

'Now in the morning, as they passed by, they saw the fig tree dried up from the roots. And Peter, remembering, said to Him, "Rabbi, look! The fig tree which you cursed has withered away." So Jesus answered and said to them, "Have faith in God. For assuredly, I say to you, whoever says to this mountain, 'Be removed and cast into the sea,' and does not doubt in his heart, but believes that those things that he says will be done, he will have whatever he says. Therefore I say to you, whatever things you ask when you pray, believe that you receive them, and you will have them."'

(Mark 11:20–24)

Imagine the headlines in the local papers in Jerusalem – **'Jesus of Nazareth kills a fig tree'**. It's an unusual thing to do, but the fact that it was God who did it is even more difficult for us to grasp. He spoke to it and it died!

What you need to know before you pray

1. Everything God speaks will happen

> '...So shall My Word be that goes forth from My mouth; it shall not return to Me void, but it shall accomplish what I please, and it shall prosper in the thing for which I sent it.'
> (Isaiah 55:11)

God's Word is far more powerful than we can understand with our finite minds – God spoke and the entire universe was formed. He sends out His Word and it does whatever it was sent to do. When Jesus spoke to sick bodies they were healed. When He spoke to the wind and waves they were calm. He says it and it comes to pass.

2. Everything God gives us to speak will come to pass

> 'Then the Lord put forth His hand and touched my mouth, and the Lord said to me: "Behold, I have put My words in your mouth. See, I have this day set you over the nations and over the kingdoms, to root out and to pull down, to destroy and to throw down, to build and to plant."' (Jeremiah 1:9–10)

Jeremiah was given God's words to speak. These words had power to tear down and build. He was given authority over the nations and kingdoms to bring God's will and purposes into the earth. Now Jesus has raised every believer to heavenly places in Him, far above every power of the enemy. He has given believers authority in His Name to tear down the enemy and build God's Kingdom **by speaking the word He gives**.

3. The fig tree demonstrates what happens when the word is spoken

Jesus only ever spoke the words His Father gave Him to speak (John 5:19). He demonstrated to His disciples that not only were people healed by His words but He also had authority and power to destroy the works of the enemy.

> ' . . . *for this purpose the Son of God was manifested, that He might destroy the works of the devil.'*   (1 John 3:8b)

We are called as believers to enforce the glorious victory that Jesus won. We have authority from God to speak directly to demonic powers and remove them. However, just as Jesus waited to hear and see what His Father was doing, so we must be led by the Spirit to speak and address the enemy. The words we speak under the guidance and anointing of the Holy Spirit will have power – to root out, tear down the enemy – and to build and plant God's Kingdom.

4. A time delay doesn't mean it hasn't happened
As soon as Jesus spoke to the tree the work in the spirit was done. Yet, the visible or natural sign didn't come until the morning when the disciples passed by and saw the dead tree. Faith believes when there's no physical evidence. When we speak God's Word it will accomplish what it was sent to do and 'in the morning' we will see the change.

5. Faith in God moves mountains
Mark 11:22 tells us to have faith **in** God so that we can move mountains and obstacles out of our way. This scripture means to actually have the faith **of** God. The faith that He supplies to us actually is His faith. We release this faith as we fill our minds and hearts with vision of Him and His Word. Looking at negative circumstances is one sure way to operate in unbelief and is the wrong focus. We have faith as we look to Him – the kind of faith that will overcome everything.

To us our faith may seem so small and insufficient but you only need tiny, mustard seed size faith to get a tremendous victory. Don't consider yourself, but consider Him and trust in Him to do it. The faith you have in Him will move any mountain.

6. What are these mountains?
Jesus was not speaking about moving natural mountains. The Swiss Alps are just fine where they are! He uses something we

can relate to in the natural world to demonstrate a truth about the spirit-world. In the natural, mountains are large and can seem almost powerful and rather intimidating. They prevent easy access or movement and may completely block the way. It takes effort and time to go over or travel around a mountain and they also restrict us from seeing what is beyond them.

It is the same with a spiritual mountain. At times there are demonic hindrances that prevent us from freely moving in the will and blessings of God. They are very real (even though we can't see them with our natural eyes) and do oppose God's people.

We can face personal mountains of fear, sickness, failure or debt, mountains of depression, unbelief or condemnation. They try to dominate our life and restrict our view of God's blessing and Kingdom purposes. God's plan is to prosper us and not to harm us, to give us a hope and a future. He has good and generous thoughts towards us, great plans for our future (see Jeremiah 29:11).

Anything that blocks the path or view of God's blessing needs to be moved. Things like intimidation, fear and poverty are from the devil. God wants us to live with His view and perspective on life. Before you can deal with the enemy, you must first have faith that God wants to bless you. This only comes from receiving the truth of His Word. Be convinced that you have a wonderful future of blessing and provision in God ahead of you.

We will need to use this command of faith not just for ourselves but also for other people to see freedom from hindrances and demonic powers (see Matthew 17:14–21).

7. Speak to your mountain – don't pray about it!

Power is released as you speak directly to the need or problem in faith. A common mistake many Christians make is that they ask God to move the mountain for them. We ourselves need to take up our position and authority in Christ and command every mountain to move, speaking out what we know to be God's will. Let the Holy Spirit lead and reveal specific mountains and then move them. This can be done in your bedroom at home – you don't necessarily have to be where the problem is. There is no distance in the Spirit. What you say at home will change your workplace or situations even in other nations. See them removed through eyes of faith.

8. Pray and receive

Jesus then teaches us to receive whatever we ask in prayer. This is a definite request for a definite answer! Be specific about what you want from Him. Many people spend so much time thinking that they are praying but never actually ask for anything. Believe that He will give whatever you ask according to His will and thank Him.

Application

1. Submit yourself to God and receive faith from His Word. Know what God wants for your life or situation. Be clear about what is *not* the will of God.

2. Ask the Lord to reveal any specific hindrances to His will. With faith in God, speak to every mountain and command them to move. 'Mountain of ... be removed and cast into the sea in Jesus' Name.' Believe in your heart that you have what you say.

3. Now pray according to His will and make a definite request. Believe that He gives what you ask and receive it from Him – by faith. Thank Him and continue to give thanks that you have received it and will see it.

   Praise the Lord – you have what you say – you have what you pray!

Prayer and fasting

Definition

To go without food for a set period of time in order to pray, seek and receive God's will.

(Fasting coupled with prayer is a powerful spiritual weapon that will overcome the powers of darkness. It also helps to subdue a believer's flesh/self-life so that more of the power and victory of God is released.)

Foundational scripture

> *'Moreover, when you fast, do not be like the hypocrites, with a sad countenance. For they disfigure their faces that they may appear to men to be fasting. Assuredly, I say to you, they have their reward. But you, when you fast, anoint your head and wash your face, so that you do not appear to men to be fasting, but to your Father who is in the secret place; and your Father who sees in secret will reward you openly.'*
>
> (Matthew 6:16–18)

(See also Matthew 17:14–21 and Isaiah 58:6–12.)

What you need to know before you fast and pray

1. Fasting releases faith and power

After Jesus was baptised in the Jordan and **filled** with the Spirit, He was led into the wilderness where He ate nothing for 40 days. Scripture records that when He returned to Galilee, a change had taken place. He returned in the **power** of the Spirit (see Luke 4:1, 14).

There is a situation recorded in Scripture where the disciples were struggling to see a boy delivered from a demon. These disciples had already seen demons submit to them in Jesus' name and people healed through their ministries. However in this situation, much to their dismay, they failed to see the victory for the child. Jesus arrived on the scene, rebuked the disciples for their unbelief, then addressed the evil spirit and set the boy free. Later when the disciples were on their own with Jesus, they asked Him why they had failed to set the boy free.

> *'So Jesus said to them, "Because of your unbelief; for assuredly I say to you, if you have faith as a mustard seed, you will say to this mountain, move from here to there, and it will move; and nothing will be impossible for you. However, this kind does not go out except by prayer and fasting."'*
>
> (Matthew 17:20–21)

The reason for their failure was unbelief. Faith will move 'mountains' but whenever victory is not seen, Jesus says we can fast and to pray so that our faith will be increased and the victory won. Jesus always operated in perfect faith and there-fore didn't need go on a fast to see this boy delivered. You and I are yet to be perfected in faith but have this weapon of great value at our disposal that will help to increase our faith.

Note: Fasting doesn't **earn** anything from God. Jesus has already accomplished everything we need through His death and resurrection. Fasting helps to release His power.

2. Jesus said 'when you fast' and not 'if'!
Jesus expects fasting to be an integral part of a believer's life. He didn't say 'if you fast', and so it's clear that we should plan it into our lifestyle, as led by the Spirit.

3. Fasting weakens our flesh in order to strengthen our spiritual life
When we give ourselves to pray and fast we are determining to make God's will and Kingdom a priority. The flesh is weakened or subdued as a result and God's Kingdom purposes become stronger within us. Our hearts become increasingly consumed with desire to see Him impact the situations we are praying for.

There are times when we need new things in our relation-ship with God. Our prayer life may become dry and not as exciting as it could be. Fasting and seeking God for a deeper revelation of Jesus will bring us into a new place with Him. As we draw near to God and give up desires for other things, He draws near to us and meets with us in new and wonderful ways.

4. Fasting and prayer brings deliverance in a crisis
The Book of Esther shows us that when the enemy is working to bring destruction, if the people of God will fast and pray together, He will bring an awesome deliverance. There is great power released through corporate fasting that can affect and deliver a nation (Esther 4:14–15). Of course, this is true for individuals who fast to see deliverance from the attack of the enemy both personally and for others.

5. Fasting and prayer for guidance and direction

There are times when as individuals and churches we need to seek God for revelation of His direction and will in our lives. As we give ourselves to Him, spirit, soul and body, He will speak and reveal His will to us (Ezra 8:21–23 and Acts 13:1–2).

6. Fast and pray with faith

Believers are to live by faith and are therefore to fast by faith. We need to be expecting God to do great things when we fast and pray. Fasting will not accomplish anything or please God unless faith is operating. Be specific and know why you are fasting and believe God for the answers.

7. A fasted life

Going without food is one thing but living a 'fasted life' for God and others is another. Isaiah 58 reveals that God is pleased with a life that gives up selfish desires, to see deliverance and healing in others. This passage of Scripture is full of the blessings that overtake us when we live to provide for the poor and needy. We are not only to fast from food but also give to others so they can receive the blessings of God. Our heart motive in all we do must be for God's glory and we will have power to see many lives transformed by His power and love.

Application

Apply wisdom in your fast and always remember to respect your body. If you have a medical problem or are unwell, please seek medical advice. If you are pregnant do not go without food but maybe give up the cream cakes!

1. A very practical decision needs to be made first – when will you fast? Make a decision to fast regularly and maybe even put it in your diary!

2. Next, determine how long the fast will be. If you haven't fasted before don't go immediately into a long fast. Start with fasting maybe one meal and then build from there to one day, three days etc. (Never fast for more than 40 days as this will damage your body.)

There is no competition and law concerning fasting. It should flow out of our loving relationship with the Lord. Do not be tempted to compare yourself with those that fast for long periods. We are not seeking man's approval but are walking in obedience to God.

3. Decide what kind of fast you are going on. Briefly, here are four biblical types of fasting:

   ▶ A complete fast – no food or drink (see Esther 4:15–16). **(Make sure you never go more than three days without water.)**

   ▶ A normal fast – no food (see Luke 4:2).

   ▶ A partial fast – with some type of food removed from your diet (see Daniel 12 – Daniel ate vegetables and no meat.)

   ▶ A corporate fast – joining together with other believers (see Ezra 8:21–23).

   I would like to add here that other things could also be fasted – like television and videos. Give the time you would normally take in leisure to pray.

4. Ask the Holy Spirit to help you fast and He will! Use any available time to pray and listen to Him. Working life often has to continue as normal, but make a special effort to spend time with God in prayer and the Word.

5. Have a purpose set in your heart when you fast. You may have one thing that you are praying for or you could have many areas where you see the need a miracle. Bring them to the Lord and tell Him you are determined and believing to see His will in these situations. Expect to hear God and see the victory.

6. Resist temptation to break the fast and try to see it right through. Your body will complain a little but don't give up. If you do fail grace always abounds. (You may decide to drink fruit juices during your fast but be careful not to use juices that are very acidic.)

   Be aware that the enemy will try to discourage you as you fast – take authority over every spirit of oppression and discouragement.

7. Fast in secret if possible. Jesus said that if we fast to impress man then we have our reward from man. But if we fast in secret before Him we will have our reward from Him (Matthew 6:16–18).

8. Be wise about how you break the fast. A huge burger and chips may appeal, but exercise self-control and wisdom.

9. Rejoice in the victory that has been won and remember that faith needs to be working even once the fast is over. God has answered and the enemy is defeated.

The prayer of intercession

Definition

The word intercession means to 'mediate' or to 'go between'. Intercession takes place whenever a believer represents a person or persons before God in prayer in order to release His mercy and will into their lives.

Note:

It is important to note here that we can never override another person's will, but our prayers do bring God's power into their lives so they are free to receive from Him.

Foundational scriptures

'So, I sought for a man among them who would make a wall, and stand in the gap before Me on behalf of the land, that I should not destroy it, but I found none.'   (Ezekiel 22:30)

'Therefore He said that He would destroy them, had not Moses His chosen one stood before Him in the breach, to turn away His wrath, lest He destroy them.'   (Psalm 106:23)

'Your kingdom come, your will be done on earth as it is in heaven.'   (Matthew 6:10)

What you need to know before you pray

1. It's not God's will to destroy the land

The prayer of intercession has power to turn an entire nation to God! Our faith and vision as we pray is to be founded on this truth that God wants to bless and have mercy on our nation and on every person alive. Our job is to pray the will of God, which is **mercy** and not judgement.

2. Intercession is for you

God is looking for intercessors so that He can accomplish His will on earth. Will you respond to His call? One believer joined with the will of God and interceding for others will bring this to pass. This is not just a call to those who have a 'special' gift of intercession. Every believer is called by God to intercede. Jesus demonstrated to us the greatest act of intercession (or mediation) by reconciling man to God through His death on the Cross. We now intercede for others by drawing on His finished work, praying in His Kingdom and enforcing His victory over the enemy.

3. Intercession brings victory over the powers of darkness

We have authority in the name of Jesus to prevent or bind the enemy's work. As we intercede the Holy Spirit may lead us to address the powers of darkness directly and enforce the victory that Jesus won.

4. Intercession changes your heart

It is more blessed to give than to receive. Praying for others enlarges our hearts and fills us with God's compassion. He loves people, and intercession for the Church and the world brings a far deeper revelation of His heart. Join with Him in this high calling and be changed.

5. Intercession changes the world

Whenever a believer prays for others, God will be working and the strategy of the enemy will be defeated. When we as the Church take on our God-given responsibility to pray for the people of our town or city there will be changes as the will and destiny of God impacts those people. God promises to heal our land when His people turn from sin, seek His face, humble themselves and pray (2 Chronicles 7:14).

6. Pray with faith

There are times in intercession where the needs and problems can overwhelm us. We need to constantly lift our eyes and hearts to Jesus. Make sure you stay in faith with victory in your heart and mind and **pray the answer and not the problem**.

Nothing is too difficult for Him and He is able to do far more than we can ask or imagine (Ephesians 3:20).

7. Understand the different expressions of the Spirit

▶ *Groaning* (Romans 8:26)

To groan means 'to voice a deep, wordless and prolonged sound expressive of grief or pain'. These sounds in prayer come from the Holy Spirit within us and are expressions too deep for us to articulate with our own language. It is different from praying in tongues. We can choose when to pray in tongues, but when this type of prayer is needed, the Spirit will lead us from normal tongues into groanings. Jesus 'groaned in the spirit and was troubled' just before Lazarus was raised from the dead (John 11:33). This type of prayer produces resurrection life and power.

▶ *Travail* (Galatians 4:19 and 1 Kings 18:41–44)

To travail means 'strenuous mental or physical exertion, tribulation, agony or anguish, and the labour of child-bearing'. In 1 Kings we see Elijah going to the top of Mount Carmel and bowing down to pray. He actually got into the same position that the women of his day used to give birth to children. Very unusual behaviour – he might have got a few comments from the locals! Elijah was praying in this way to give birth to the will of God. The natural position reflected what was happening in the Spirit to release the promised miracle of rain. He was labouring with the Holy Spirit, just like a woman will yield in labour to birth her child. Travail gives birth to miracles.

Another time we see this mentioned in the New Testament when Paul began to 'travail' again in prayer for believers (Galatians 4:19). He had obviously used this type of prayer to initially birth them into the Kingdom, but now the purpose was to bring them to maturity. Praying this way brings souls into the Kingdom and brings believers to maturity.

▶ *Tears* (Psalm 126:5–6)

This is sometimes referred to as 'liquid prayer'. As we are interceding for others God may touch our hearts with His compassion so powerfully that we will weep. Jesus wept over Jerusalem and also just before Lazarus was raised from the dead. The Holy Spirit will use your tears in prayer. The ground of people's hearts will soften as we pray with tears. This intercession is powerful and will produce a spiritual harvest.

Application

> *'Likewise the Spirit helps in our weaknesses. For we do not know what we should pray for as we ought, but the Spirit Himself makes intercession for us with groanings which cannot be uttered.'*   (Romans 8:26)

1. Ask the Holy Spirit to fill you and lead you into effective intercession. He will show you what to pray and will intercede through you with different sounds and expressions.

2. Pray with faith. If you are unsure of His will, ask the Lord to reveal it to you from His Word.

3. As you pray for others there will be different things that the Holy Spirit will want to accomplish. Yield and move into different kinds of prayer and expressions. Be free to flow with what God is doing.

4. Pray until you know the work has been done. Most of the intercession we do is not just a one-time prayer but is usually for a season. Pray as you are led. The Lord will make it clear when to stop. Sometimes it's obvious because the answer arrives. Other times the Lord will have us carry a burden for His will in prayer for days, weeks or even years. Stay in faith.

5. Heaviness, oppression and negativity are from the devil and are not the will of God. Take authority over every evil spirit that may be operating against you. Submit to God, resist the devil and he will flee from you (James 4:7).

6. Rejoice in the Lord always! As you are interceding you will experience God's love and compassion. You may feel anguish and sadness during the prayer but you must finish in faith and victory. Rejoice in the Lord and keep your eyes on Him.

Praying with perseverance

Definition

In this type of prayer a believer has a determination, that comes from knowing the will of God, to continue to pray and not give up until the answer comes.

Foundational scripture

> 'And He said to them, "Which of you shall have a friend, and go to him at midnight and say to him, 'Friend, lend me three loaves; for a friend of mine has come to me on his journey, and I have nothing to set before him'; and he will answer from within and say, 'Do not trouble me; the door is now shut, and my children are with me in bed; I cannot rise and give to you'? I say to you, though he will not rise and give to him because he is his friend, yet because of his persistence he will rise and give him as many as he needs. So, I say to you, ask, and it will be given to you; seek, and you will find; knock, and it will be opened to you. For everyone who asks receives, and he who seeks finds, and to him who knocks it will be opened."' (Luke 11:5–10)

What you need to know before you pray

1. Insist on an answer

Jesus teaches us through this scripture that friendship was not enough to supply the need. It was an almost annoying perseverance that won the day! At times we need to go beyond the boundaries of 'friendly and sociable' prayer to a bold insistence to possess our rights as sons of God (Galatians 4:7).

This is not irreverent and neither is it presumption. We ask based on what we know is available to us from the Word of God. At times, Jesus will give our requests only when we become determined to get what we are asking for. We must exercise our position as sons and boldly keep knocking until we receive.

2. Boldness comes from knowing His will

We will not be able to persevere in prayer unless the Holy Spirit has revealed God's will to us from Scripture. With this determination birthed in us by Him we can go before His throne knowing that He will answer us. We know that He has said it and so we can insist that He does it.

3. Different stages in persevering prayer

▶ *'Ask, and you will receive.'*

This is simply asking God based on His promises. The scripture here means to ask and go on asking. Repetition is right and good as long as the prayer continues in faith! (Unbelief asks repeatedly for something and wonders if God will answer.) You may receive the answer immediately. If not, be prepared and willing to continue.

▶ *'Seek, and you will find.'*

The prayer enters a new stage and becomes stronger and more earnest. There is a new determination to receive the answer. During this time the Lord may change your heart-motive to refine the prayer so that what is left is the pure will of God. If there is anything hindering the prayer, the Lord will reveal it as we seek Him. He may reveal other areas that need prayer, which will release your answer.

▶ *'Knock, and it will be opened to you.'*

Knock and go on knocking until the door is opened. At this stage we have gone beyond 'it would be nice to see this happen' to 'this **must** happen'. Holy boldness takes over and you have one target and one aim – to get what you ask for. This prayer will often be loud. Constant knocking on a door to get an answer can be noisy!

Remember that we are not twisting God's arm but are praying for His will. He loves this kind of determination in prayer. Persist, don't give up, and the door will open for you.

Application

1. Before you pray, know what you want and make sure it agrees with God's will.

2. Let the Holy Spirit empower you to keep persevering with determination.

3. Ask and go on asking. Seek and go on seeking. Knock and go on knocking. Become increasingly urgent and insistent in your prayers. Like Jacob – *'I will not let you go unless you bless me!'* (Genesis 32:26).

4. Jesus told us not to lose heart and always to pray (Luke 18:1–8). He knew we would be tempted to give up before we receive the answer. Keep your hope firmly in the Lord and His promises and refuse discouragement. For situations such as praying for our cities and nation we must continue to persevere until we see what the Lord has promised.

   'In due season we shall reap if we do not lose heart.'
   (Galatians 6:9)

Chapter 7

Church Prayer –
What Should Happen!

The power of corporate prayer

Something exciting is happening in the worldwide church of
Jesus Christ. The revelation of the local church praying
together is being restored and prayer meetings are becoming
like the ones we read about in the book of Acts. Everyone is
praying together, all at the same time, in one heart and mind
in agreement with God. The result is that God's power is
shaking the world.

God not only calls His people to pray individually but also
corporately. More believers are catching the vision for this
and are beginning to take responsibility for the corporate
prayer life of the Church. We see from Scripture that this is
how the Lord intends it to be.

> **Corporate prayer is today changing
> cities and nations**

As local churches gather together and pray the awesome
power of God is being released on earth, often in ways that
are taking people by surprise. I have recently read reports that
many Muslims have converted to Christ after receiving
visions and dreams about Jesus. The Lord is pouring out His
Spirit in answer to prayer and the end-time harvest of souls is

being reaped in all nations. As we ask, the Lord sends out labourers into the harvest fields and entire nations, which have historically resisted the gospel, are beginning to yield and respond to Jesus.

United to pray

We know that in order to fulfil God's plan, every believer needs to develop a strong, personal prayer life. However, we cannot accomplish His purposes for our lives alone. We need to be part of a local church so that together we can pray and work to see God's plans fulfilled, both personally and corporately. Although each believer has an important ministry given by God, there is a higher revelation that we need to receive and walk in. Our personal ministry must be integrated with and serve the ministry of the local church. United we will see God's plans and destiny for our church, area, city and nation.

Prayer brings people together in heart and purpose. We are already united in Christ, but will continue to be strengthened in our call together as we pray. A people who pray together will have power to overcome obstacles and trials and will have spiritual understanding of the purposes of God. A praying church will be a powerful church.

Not only do individual believers have a responsibility to give themselves to corporate prayer, but church leadership must seek God and learn how to lead people into exciting Spirit-led prayer. It's the Spirit who gives life – the flesh profits nothing (John 6:63). People will not want to be there if the meeting is boring and full of man-made agendas.

As we give ourselves to the work of prayer the Holy Spirit will do wonders through us.

Foundational scriptures

> 'When the Day of Pentecost had fully come, they were all with one accord in one place.'   (Acts 2:1)

> '...they raised their voice to God with one accord and said...'   (Acts 4:24)

> *'Again I say to you that if two of you agree on earth*
> *concerning anything that they ask, it will be done for them*
> *by My Father in heaven.'*   (Matthew 18:19)

Before the outpouring of the promised Holy Spirit at Pentecost the believers were together in one accord. To be in one accord is not just an agreement of mind but also of purpose. They were in harmony with God and one another and were waiting for the 'Promise of the Father' (Acts 1:4–5).

The Holy Spirit came in power, the Church was born and the world was turned upside down! To be in one accord has great significance for the Church. Throughout history we see that God has poured out His Spirit as His people seek Him together and pray with a common purpose in mind.

A famous soft drinks company has a 'mission' statement, which aims to get a bottle of their product into the hands of every person in the world. Their mission isn't just to England or Europe – it's the world. I've travelled to some of the poorest nations where the people lack the basic necessities, yet they do have a bottle of this well-known drink. A common purpose will unite, strengthen and bring success to a people, even in the secular world. This is what needs to happen in our church prayer meetings as we come together with a common purpose.

In Acts 4:24 we read of another prayer meeting where the believers were praying with one accord – in harmony once again with the heart, mind and purpose of God. They received what they were asking with such power that even the building they were in was physically shaken (Acts 4:31).

The truth is that whenever the Church comes together in this way, great victories will be secured. The early Church was unstoppable and constantly expanding as God's power was released through their prayers.

We see another important key in Acts 4:24. They all lifted their voice and prayed out aloud – all at the same time. It was noisy, but it was a heavenly sound!

Coming into a corporate prayer meeting for the first time without understanding what is going on can be difficult. I remember the first time I experienced this kind of prayer meeting. I was so full of my own 'culture' and didn't want to pray too loud or be noticed by anyone. I felt so awkward as I watched others who were lost in the prayer. The Lord had to change me and show me that this is the way He wants His Church to pray. Quite a shock to my system! Once I had the revelation from His Word though, I too could enter into this wholeheartedly.

Think of an orchestra again. The sound wouldn't be right if the violin section went on strike and wouldn't play. And if the percussion played a different section, then there would be chaos! Corporate prayer needs everyone to be praying with one common theme in mind. Each person in harmony with the Lord and each other, adding their prayer of faith.

Just as an orchestra needs a conductor, so too a corporate prayer meeting needs clear direction through an anointed leader. This enables everyone to enter into the prayer with one heart and mind.

What is accomplished through corporate prayer?

(Please see 'The prayer of agreement' in Chapter 6.)

1. 'One heart and one mind' produces strength in the church

Praying together brings people into the revelation of God's will. Every local church is given specific vision from God, which the leaders need to communicate to the people. If the church pray that vision together, the Lord will set it firmly into hearts and people will become one in heart and mind. This unity of purpose will bring God's presence and power into the church, with everyone moving together in the same direction. Weakness enters the Body whenever there is division and differences in vision and purpose. Strength comes as we walk together in God's purposes.

2. Awesome power is released

The church agreeing in prayer brings a supernatural increase in power. Deuteronomy 32:30 tells us that one puts a thousand to flight, two ten thousand. Whole communities will be impacted by His presence and power as we pray together.

3. Awesome authority is released

God has given authority to the church to rule in His Name over every principality, power and ruler of darkness. Led by the Holy Spirit, we come into agreement together and bind every evil spirit that is hindering the advancement of the Kingdom of God. The local church should take responsibility for their area or city, rule over the works of the enemy and loose the Kingdom of God.

4. Destiny is fulfilled as the church persists in prayer

A praying church will loose the destiny of God over individuals, cities and nations. In Acts 12:1–17, Peter was chained and put in prison because of his faith. The church got together and prayed **constantly** for him. God sent an angel to free him from his chains so that he could go on and continue to fulfil God's purposes. The enemy wants to stop the fruitfulness of both individuals and the church, but prayer will loose God's power and keep us free to serve Him and do His will.

5. A praying church will be a going church

A praying church will be a church of mission and action. The Lord will do a work in our hearts as we pray, bringing desire and vision to go and fulfil the great commission – to make disciples of all nations for Jesus (Matthew 28:18–20).

How to have effective corporate prayer meetings

Here are some key points that will help us to be effective in corporate prayer meetings:

1. We have come to pray

This may be obvious but the purpose for a prayer meeting is to pray and receive answers from God. There is a time for fellowship, for preaching etc., but we need to guard this time and make sure that our prayer meetings are full of prayer. It may be right at times to hear a short word from Scripture to minister faith and direction, or to minister to the Lord in worship and praise, but we must pray. Don't let this time be stolen!

2. Every believer submitted to God

We each must be right with God before we pray. Allow time
for people to confess any sin and receive the cleansing power
of His blood, releasing His presence and grace. Each person
must be willing to give himself to the corporate flow of prayer.
When we are alone with God we are free to go wherever He
leads us personally. Corporate prayer is different in that we
must lay aside our own agendas and willingly go with the
corporate anointing and direction. Refusing to go with this or
the appointed leader of the meeting will break the power of
agreement and decrease the effectiveness of the prayer.

3. Everyone filled with the Spirit

The power and enabling in prayer will come from the Holy
Spirit. Together, we can each ask to be filled and receive by
faith.

4. Flow together as one

Praying in the Spirit is a bit like being in a river that can
change pace and direction very quickly. We need to be
flexible and move into the unknown and sometimes 'un-
charted' territory by faith. Agreement is where the power is
and so we need to keep in the same flow of the Spirit
together. If the Lord says 'pray for the government' to the
leader, then he or she will communicate this to everyone and
we can all begin to pray together. We can't have someone
deciding to intercede for India when the rest of us are praying
for the government in England. Maybe the Lord will lead
everyone into prayer for India later. The key is to remember
that we are to have one heart and mind in this kind of prayer
and we need to stay submitted to His purposes.

Whilst praying, individuals may receive prophetic visions,
interpretation or words from God. During corporate prayer
they are to pray out to the Lord what they are seeing without
interrupting the corporate flow. There can be time for feed-
back afterwards.

5. The faith dynamic

During corporate prayer, the Lord will at times lift us
together into a greater dynamic of faith. There is a specific

anointing of faith released by the Holy Spirit upon the whole body to believe God for awesome things. When this happens, we need to act and ask for the things we can believe for. According to our faith it will be done. It can seem like the Lion of Judah is being released and nothing is impossible for us. We have supernatural power and faith that will change nations. What wonderful and exciting prayer! We leave these prayer meetings knowing that God has done great things.

6. Praise and worship
At times the Holy Spirit will lead to us into worship and praise. This can happen before we begin to pray or even during the prayer meetings. Scripture tells us that the Lord inhabits the praises of His people (Psalm 22:3). This literally means He comes to 'sit down, settle or marry'. Wherever the Lord is, there is no darkness or oppression. As we worship He will manifest His presence amongst us and from this place of intimacy together with Him we can be easily led into the prayer that is on His heart. A people who are focused on Jesus will start and continue with the right perspective in prayer.

There is a type of prayer which is mentioned over 70 times in Scripture called 'tephillah' – which is sung prayer (2 Chronicles 6:20). At times this may be appropriate for us to do together. Led by the Spirit, we can sing prophetic songs and prayers of deliverance over people and nations.

Psalm 149 tells us that the Lord defeats the enemy and binds powers of darkness as His people declare His praise and proclaim His Word. There are changes that take place in the spirit-world as we praise and worship God. Where Light comes, darkness must flee.

The prayer leader

1. Whoever leads must be anointed
An anointed prayer leader will be able to bring the whole body together into prayer in the Spirit. Always remember that it is God who chooses and anoints people for specific tasks and not man! Every leader in the church can pray but we mustn't automatically assume that every leader can lead corporate prayer. It's the same principle with worship

leading. Everyone can worship but few can bring the whole body into worship. It's an anointing from the Holy Spirit that enables this to happen.

Identify those with leadership qualities and anointed by God to lead prayer.

2. He or she must live in heart submission to the church leadership

In order to have the corporate dynamic in prayer the leader(s) must have the same vision and heart as the church leader. They don't have to know all the details about the church but they do need to be loyal and faithful in serving the church and the leadership.

3. The leader must have a personal prayer life

You can only give what you have. If you are called to lead prayer you must have a strong and disciplined personal prayer life.

4. The leader must be strong in the Word

To lead prayer, the will of God must be known from His Word. This will produce faith and confidence that God will answer prayer according to His Word. There also needs to be evidence or fruit of a life of faith from that person. If the prayer leader can't believe God for their personal lives – then how can they lead the church to believe God?

5. The gift of encouragement

The prayer leader needs to be an encourager of people. The leader needs to be able to flow with God and to encourage the people to follow in faith. I personally think that this has to be one of the main gifts in leading prayer. People don't always need to be told what is wrong with their praying but need encouragement into what is right.

How to lead corporate prayer

Here are some important keys to leading corporate prayer. This is definitely not all there is to know, but I do hope it will give some useful guidelines.

1. Preparation

Before a prayer meeting the leader should spend time with the Lord in the Word and prayer. The Lord may give some specific direction for the prayer meeting but in my experience, it will not normally be in detail. The main thing that happens in this time is heart preparation. We must be 'in tune' with God and filled with the Spirit and Word to lead prayer.

If you have no understanding of what the Lord wants to do in the prayer meeting ask for the gift of faith. It's like walking on water out there and you need to have faith that He won't let you sink.

At times the church leadership may give you things that you need to pray about. Take these before the Lord and ask Him to help you direct and lead this specific prayer with revelation.

Don't over-prepare, and go in His peace.

2. Begin to lead

Begin the meeting by giving direction to the people. Maybe start by allowing the people to put their hearts and lives right with God and thank Him together for His blood. You may want to introduce a time of worship and praise. Just be sensitive to the Lord. Bring everyone together with the focus on Jesus, minister faith and begin praying.

3. Be aware of the Lord *and* the people

It's no good if you and the Lord are having a great time but you've left everyone else watching. Your job is to encourage them into the prayer. If you need to stop and minister faith or give understanding, then do. We must all be involved together.

Can I emphasise here that to lead you have to follow the Lord and not the people! A prayer meeting must please God and not the flesh! At times the people may seem uninterested or even unwilling to follow. Don't give up and stop, but build faith and bring them on.

4. Be willing to change direction

It will be necessary to move with the Spirit into different directions and different kinds of prayer. Lead the people by example and don't get stuck in the rut of method or style. If you are using a microphone be sensitive to the amount you use it. If the leader talks too much others can be put off praying. If he talks too little the prayer can lack faith or direction. Practice and experience will show you what works and what doesn't.

5. Have faith no matter what!

The enemy will attack and try to bring doubt and fear as you are leading but keep your eyes on Jesus and use the Word in prayer. Do everything for God's glory and believe that God has answered the prayers of the people.

Note: One way to start a meeting and get everyone flowing together in one heart and mind is to all pray a particular scripture out aloud. This will increase everyone's faith and give clear direction and understanding of God's will.

Group prayer

Praying in smaller groups is also an important part of the prayer life of the church. There are some things that need to be carried by the whole body in prayer, but at times smaller groups are the most effective way to pray and bring about God's victory and will.

Small groups can have their own 'identity', which usually comes through certain individuals sharing a common vision. For example, a group of people may share a burden to see the gospel preached in a local prison. This group may have some members working in evangelism or pastoral care within the prison. When they meet together to pray for the work, they have a heart for the people and will understand their needs. They will then be able to accurately target the individual and specific needs in prayer.

It is so important to understand the dynamic of group prayer. There are spiritual principles that need to be applied in every group to fulfil God's will for the group. Just as we saw with corporate prayer, we must have unity and agreement together if we are to accomplish all that God wants. Here are some comments and observations that will help to increase fruitfulness for group prayer.

Keys to leading group prayer

1. Group submitted to church leadership and vision

Every prayer group will operate in authority if they are submitted to God's appointed authority in the church. God's order is clearly established through His choice of church leadership and groups are to be careful to submit to that authority. This means that the prayer group will be in harmony with the pastor and the vision of the local church. Then the Lord will command the blessing and there will be an ease and flow in prayer.

There are of course situations where Christians from all denominations are meeting in workplaces and agreeing in prayer. Power in prayer will come from their heart submission to the Lord and one another.

2. Leadership within the group

Someone needs to be responsible to lead the group. Without leadership, the prayer time can become full of everyone's opinions or requests and the group may never enter fully into the will of God.

Of course, whoever is chosen needs to have an anointing to lead, together with a heart to serve. They are to be submitted to the corporate vision, teachable and faithful. They also need to have a life of prayer and faith so that they can lead by example.

The leader must have a clear vision for the purpose of that group and they need to be able to impart that vision to the people in the group. If the prayer goes off track they need to bring it back in love, but firmly. Of course, the leader is not to control or dominate the group but facilitate and release others to pray and be led by the Spirit.

It is important that there is some level of communication between the prayer group leader and pastor. This really helps to keep everything in the light and in submission. The pastor can then if appropriate feed in needs for prayer that will assist the whole ministry of the church.

Please note:

Intercession groups can become vulnerable to elitism, spiritual pride and manipulation. Be aware that the enemy would love to hijack the prayer in this way and so be careful to stay humble, teachable and submitted to church leadership. Keep in mind that the leader of the church is called by God to lead the church and not the intercessors. Intercessors are called to help, assist and encourage the vision of leadership through Spirit-led prayer. Keep a pure heart and motive and there will be grace operating in the group to pray mightily for the glory of God. Remember God opposes the proud, but gives grace to the humble (James 4:6).

3. In one accord

There needs to be a heart and mind agreement in every individual if we are to be effective through group prayer (see notes on corporate prayer). For example, one person can't keep praying for children when the leader of the group is leading prayer for old people. Personal agendas have to yield to the Lord's agenda for the group.

4. Use different kinds of prayer

The Holy Spirit does not want the prayer to become stale but will minister faith and vision to the people. There needs to be a freedom in the group to move into many different kinds of prayer and to operate in the gifts of the Spirit. Always praying the same way can become a method. Prayer is full of life if it's Spirit-led.

5. Flowing together

Each member is to be sensitive both to the Lord and to others in the group. We can only agree together if we can hear what someone else is praying. Listen to whoever is praying out something in their own language so that you can agree with them. To keep the flow of prayer going, everyone else can be praying in tongues whilst that person is praying, but not so loud that they can't hear the prayer. The gifts of the Spirit will operate in the group if there is freedom and faith. One may have a word of knowledge or a prophetic word. We need to listen and discern to see if it's from God. This is where it is important that the leader affirms what God is saying and leads everyone to pray the will of God. Visions may be given by the Spirit and again need to be tested and in the flow of what God is doing.

If there is an environment of love and correct order then the group will grow and develop together in powerful prayer.

6. Teaching
At times the leader may need to teach on one kind of prayer or bring a scripture to reveal the will of God and release faith. This is important, but it is not to take up too much time. The purpose of the group is to pray.

There also needs to be freedom to spend time in praise and worship as this will help bring everyone together to focus on Jesus and bring His presence. At times the group may experience spiritual heaviness or oppression from the enemy and praising the Lord will bring the victory.

7. Faith
If the group is in unbelief with a situation, stop the prayer and get the focus back on Jesus – the answer. Find a promise from Scripture and minister faith. Proclaim His victory and greatness. Pray the Word together and come back to strong confident faith in God.

8. Perseverance
Encourage one another to pray until you see the answer. Some promises that God has given will take years before we see the fulfilment. Keep growing in faith. Of course, at times there will be immediate answers to prayer. But certain prayers need determined persistence.

Always expect God to work miracles and bring testimonies of answered prayer to the group, which will encourage faith.

9. Thanksgiving and praise
End every meeting by giving thanks to God for His faithfulness. He hears and answers our prayers. Receive His victory over every circumstance and praise Him. Always keep the right focus and perspective – **Jesus reigns!**